Write Dumb

Writing Better by Thinking Less

By James Dowd

Forewarning:

1. This was entirely uncalled for.

2. Everything you're about to read is really dumb.

3. There is a writing challenge at the end, which I recommend taking before you read, *and* after, to see how the dumb tips, tricks, and techniques helped. Sorry to add more work to this reading experience.

4. While often direct, I offer all of this advice not as an authoritarian, but as a dumb Writer who made enough mistakes to know this is what works for this one dumb Writer. Use some, use all, use none, it's entirely up to you.

5. While not all of this advice will work with your learning style, do one thing: Start Stupid. Be open to new ideas, without judgement or self-consciousness, because that's the only way to truly write.

"We don't read and write poetry because it's cute.

We read and write poetry because we are members of the

human race.

And the human race is filled with passion.

Medicine, law, business, engineering — these are noble pursuits

and necessary to sustain life. But poetry, beauty, romance, love

— these are what we stay alive for. To quote from Whitman:

O me! O life! of the questions of these recurring,

Of the endless trains of the faithless, of cities fill'd with the

foolish

What good amid these, O me, O life?

Answer:

That you are here — that life exists, and identity,

That the powerful play goes on, and you may contribute a verse.

That the powerful play goes on, and *you* may contribute a verse.

What will your verse be?"

> — Tom Schulman & Walt Whitman

> by way of Dead Poet's Society

Preface: Everyone Can Write, But Not Everyone is a Writer

"Words are sacred. They deserve respect.

If you get the right ones, in the right order,

you can nudge the world a little."

— Tom Stoppard

Whether you write professionally or not, you might have heard the phrase, "Everyone can write, but not everyone is a Writer." And, if you haven't heard it, you might have felt it. It's a common phrase in the writing world that's used shut people out, to lessen their opinions and abilities, and to prevent the Writer in all of us from coming out to play.

I find it regularly used by Writers as a way to defend their jobs, their craft, and their perceived amount of respect deserved of them and their work in their respective industry while more and more people, positions, and products, like writing bots, encroach on their livelihood.

That certainly doesn't mean this notion is true. Everyone can write, therefore everyone is a Writer. It's that simple.

Even if you wanted to argue that not *everyone* can write, I'd argue that the scribbling of shapes and symbols to express and communicate is all writing is, and therefore it's not as precious a craft as many would lead us to believe.

As a paid and practiced Writer, I can confidently say that those who use this obstructive phrase feel they must defend their position because they're threatened, intimidated, and scared. After all, they sacrificed so much to get here. They dreamed, they read, they scratched, they studied, they *wrote*, especially when so many others didn't. They honed and cherished their craft. They furiously worked for the right skills, for the right jobs, in the right markets, in the right industries. They're a Writer, with a capital W. This is who they are. This is what they do. This is what they always dreamed of. And yet, common belief is that because everyone out there studied the English language for many years in school, in the U.S. at least, we're all fully equipped to be a Writer — to critique, edit, and even write in a professional capacity. How dare you, how dare I, how dare we try to capitalize that W and be a Writer, too! How dare we try to express ourselves and better communicate with the world around us! How dare we over-step our bounds, to try to be something that excites and betters us! Absurdity, for sure. However, that's exactly why all of us must approach it with care. Because while surely every one of us trained to write in some capacity, solely based on the fact that we studied it for so many years, it can still be one of the hardest things any of us will do in our daily lives. It's still expressing ourselves, and therefore exposing and revealing ourselves, our careers, our emotions, our intentions, our humanity — all frightening things to open to the world; to allow others to see us for who and what we really are.

And, sure, to be a Writer takes years of experience and training — something to measure and defend. In fact, there's a belief that being a Writer is something you must be highly skilled in, or that you have extensive education and world experience to guide your pen. But, the truth is, great writing usually comes from comfortably stripping away these things. It takes simplicity, and care, and unique personal experiences. It takes time, not talent. It takes passion, energy, and blood — all things each and every one of us possess. And that's why, when we do it right, when it feels like we're not only making progress, but making a connection with the page, and our readers, it's incredible! It's human. It's an emotional bridge to our reader, and a personal sense of freedom. That's a drug everyone has tasted and looks forward to. That's why we look toward being a Writer, or at the very least be better at it.

Remember also that job title in no way determines one's skill as a Writer. Above all else, the simple yet momentous act of writing stands alone as the greatest attribute of any writer — doing, not talking. Writing, not thinking about writing. One of the best writers I know is not a Writer by trade. He's never officially been paid for it, and his name has never been on anything publically. Yet, I anxiously await everything he writes and get excited for his new works, far more so than most "professional" writers. His name is Chris Hunt. He's an advertising executive, and not on the creative side. He's an account rep, a strategist and relationship manager. Emails and PowerPoint presentations are the only areas he's allowed to stretch and flex his writing muscles at work, but afterwards, when he's in his own world, he writes. He writes TV shows, YA novels, and musicals — all brilliant! None of them have been produced or published, which has more to say about the industries' barriers of entry than his skills, because every piece Sings! He puts his heart into every word and does the most important thing any Writer can do: he writes, he just writes. He doesn't tell people about his ideas, or spin his wheels on drafts. He writes and shares with his friends, always opening himself up for critique and failure and, through it all, evolution of his craft. He doesn't do it for fame or riches. He's a Writer. And, when the universe aligns itself and the good ones succeed, you will see his name in lights. Let that be a reminder that it is not your title that matters, or what currently pays the bills. All that matters is what you bring to the page. To be a Writer you must write. Write, share, learn, repeat. That's all there is to it. Your education is certainly enough, and don't let anyone tell you otherwise. There is no other great secret. Just don't try to be Hemingway. Try to be Hunt instead.

Keep in mind though that a Writer's plea to "non-Writers" to stay in their own lanes, to focus on their own jobs, is merely a demonstration of their broken confidence. We Writers tend to be feeble, self-conscious beasts. Our sensitivity gives us our powers. Our thirst to know more, to feel more, to have more, to be more, fuels us and inspires us. And yet, it leaves a nerve exposed for the world to pester—to torture! This exposure leaves us always open for attack, and for the opportunity to feel inferior. And so we lash out. Be prepared.

A close friend and fellow Writer, Jason Rose, once perfectly defined the life of a Writer with the bourbon-fueled comment, "Writing is torture, but great writing...that's masturbation." This epic line demonstrates how we Writers are tortured, exhausted, and constantly seeking self-pleasure. It explains the defense of the mantle of Writer, the struggles both internally and externally, and how we have very little capacity for criticism. However, it also explains why we keep doing it. It describes that high you get from putting your thoughts, ideas, and feelings onto the page — that sense of incomparable personal expression. But, despite that lovely high, it takes practice to be able to live and work in a world that actively seeks to edit and critique us, to take our precious drug away with an opposing opinion. It takes patience to hear the thoughts of others, to turn a solo exercise into a group one. And it takes a miracle to forgo your self-gratification for even a moment of agreement or accommodation, or to consider that there are now others in the world fighting for that same measly taste of our drug.

That in no way excuses those who would say "Everyone can write, but not everyone is a Writer." Writers, while skilled, experienced, and hopefully talented, are still, and will always be, subject to feedback and criticism. They're not free from it solely by the fact that they accomplished the act of writing *something*. After all, this is both a job and an art form, and therefore subject to review and opinion. Plus, the Writer may just be suffering from the IKEA Effect, which is that psychological phenomenon that allows one to believe their work is great just because they alone crafted it, much like that IKEA furniture you painstakingly put together. While done, it still might look like cheap particleboard garbage easily found in a frat guy's apartment. And so, our charge is not to fight but to check our egos, absorb everything, learn from everyone, expand our way of thinking, and to continue moving forward to our next hit. That's how we became Writers to begin with.

It certainly won't be easy, though. The pursuit and effort of writing *will* make you a Writer, but as Jason Rose also says over bourbon, "Writing is 10% skill, 40% hard work, and 50% crippling self-doubt." It's easy to critique and even harder to take critique, because the act alone exposes you to the world. Writing is a scary journey, and while some say you aren't worthy simply by taking English classes in school, they're wrong. Because you can write, you can be a Writer, regardless of what they may say. Just remember something: Great writing is not a series of words spelled correctly and lain flat within a set of strict guidelines. It's not of a certain character count. It's not done by committee. And it's certainly not meaningless.

No, great writing is music. It's both painful and glorious. It melds words and phrases in such a way as to educate and inform while making you feel as if you're part of a rare, deep, disruptive conversation. It hooks you, pushes you, and pulls you. It etches itself into your subconscious, maybe forever.

Great writing connects emotionally. It lays obstacles and shows you the way over. It excites you, and incites you. It's a skill, and an art form. It requires talent, experience, audacity, grit, and creativity. Even more, it requires empathy — the ability to feel and understand what someone else is feeling and experiencing. From habit to impulse and dedication to craving, if you can understand it, you can predict it. If you can predict it, you can provoke it. If you can make your readers feel something, they don't need to think about anything, and that's magical.

Everyone can write, but not everyone is a Writer. However, this does not mean you yourself can't be a Writer.

And, none of this means you aren't one already. Simply respect the craft. Then, be fearless and, despite all of this, never overthink it. Don't let your own criticism or self-imposed limitations stand in your way. Stop thinking so much and laugh at your own inabilities, inferiorities, and inhibitions, and at that point, no one can stop you. Think of the reader and give them an experience. Take your drug and feed their habit while you're at it.

You may say who am I to be a Writer, to put my heart and soul onto the page, to write my name on things, to have the gall to think I could stand alone with my words, to take chances, to try? I say, who the hell are you not to? This is a gift we all possess, an art we can practice without advanced instruction, a form of communication that can not only reach masses but also exist forever in time. Who are you to deny such a gift? You can write, and no one else is stopping you from being a Writer, only yourself. So don't allow yourself to stand in the way of something so fulfilling.

Everyone can write, but not everyone is a Writer.

Except, if you put yourself into it, truly. If you write with passion, energy, empathy, and truth, you're a Writer — capital W. So, please, take these techniques found in this book as a challenge to write whenever the opportunity arises, no matter who you are or what you do for a living. I promise you, it will rarely be easy, but it will always be fulfilling.

Go, be a Writer and use your words as weapons to change the way people live their lives, including your own.

Introduction:
Stop Overthinking It

"Remember how long you have procrastinated, and how consistently you have failed to put to good use your suspended sentence from the gods. It is about time you realized the nature of the universe (of which you are part) and of the power that rules it (to which your art owes its existence). Your days are numbered. Use them to throw open the windows of your soul to the sun. If you do not, the sun will soon set, and you with it."

— Marcus Aurelius

Everyone's a Writer. That's why we're here.

From writing simple everyday emails, texts, and social posts all the way to the big, time-consuming blog posts, movies, and novels that entertain the world at the end of the day, everyone's a Writer because writing is a crucial tool in our everyday lives. Whether consciously or unconsciously, all of our other communication tactics are practiced and evolved each day,

yet the moment we graduate from school, we do our best to

limit our writing, running from it, even when we have something

valuable to share, something important to express. Even our

everyday text messages have become a sad display of writing,

because what? We're too busy to use punctuation, or full words,

or anything close to correct grammar? It's usually because we're

lazy, distracted, and scared, not because we're incapable.

We make excuses. We say to ourselves, I don't know

what to create. I don't know what to say. I don't know what to

write. I don't know *how* to write it. Someone else should do it.

Someone else could do it better. I don't have the time. I can't

slow my brain down long enough. The result is

underperformance at work, inability to expand on personal

dreams and desires, as well as stilted personal communications

and, subsequently, relationships.

Words, you say them and they float off into nothingness,

but writing...it lasts, it persists, it's undying, it's you, and that

scares the ever living shit out of us. Writing is exposing your nerves, your thoughts, your feelings, your true self in an

enduring form, so you must run as far as you can from it,

because if you put any words down on paper or pixel, the world

is bound to find out who you really are. And that is the most

frightening thing we face in our daily lives — to be vulnerable, to

be naked, to be revealed.

I see the fear every day, and have for nearly two decades

as a professional Writer. I see that it's not a struggle maintained

by only those with "Writer" in their job title, or those dreaming

up their screenplays at the coffee shop. Writing is an everyday

challenge for all of us, and it's guaranteed to invite failure in

some form at some time, so we either accept that, try and fail, or

we don't even try at all. We leave it for someone else, making

excuses and continuing to run from the challenge. Or, we try

and try and try, never getting anywhere with our efforts because

we get in our own way. We think too much and feel too little,

letting our fear and over-analysis paralyze us. You've seen them,

and probably have been them. They're the never-tries and the

never-finishes. They never launched that brilliant business

because they couldn't even write the business plan. They never got the date because they couldn't think of something clever to say in that dating app. They never got the job because they just sent a resume and moved on. All of these are people who rationalize giving up or not even trying as an acceptable path away from their fears and self-doubts, when just thinking less and writing more was the true path forward.

Even for those brave souls that do try, and even those that do finish, and do publish, writing still remains an everyday challenge, owned and experienced by everyone who makes any effort at stringing together words, but I have found the simple solutions that work for them, and everyone else. For those stranded on the ends of the spectrum — the ones afraid to try on one end, and the ones unable to finish on the other — there is an answer to your writing woes, and it can be summed up into one phrase for all of you:

"You're overthinking it."

— said by me, every single day while shaking my head.

Everyone overthinks writing. You overthink it at work when you're writing even the most basic emails. You overthink it when texting. You overthink it by comparing your work to Hemingway (you're not). You overthink it and then tell yourself that that's your writing process (it's not). You overthink it when you think it's an impossible feat. You believe thought is the fuel for words, even though it's actually the one thing fueling your inability to get those words on the page.

"Writer" is a professional title many dream of bearing, and a craft that can bring one's life meaning, excitement, adventure, and riches. For others, it's not at all. Some just want to be able to write a simple damn email better, and that's why they're here. Regardless of your job, need, experience, or dreams, writing is and always will be an integral form of everyday communication that drives us personally and professionally. And yet, we're all still just overthinking the whole damn thing. It's so much simpler than anyone realizes. You're just overthinking it.

Writing is one of our strongest and most valuable tools we have to interact with this world, and yet we overthink it constantly because it scares us, it intimidates us, it challenges us, it makes us feel uncomfortable, and no one wants that nervous, *I could fuck this up and look stupid* feeling all day, every day. We don't fully understand it or feel comfortable experiencing it, so we waste time trying to add structure and rules and meaning and restrictions where they're not needed, or we altogether keep our distance. We blame the rules, or the endless possibilities, or the competition, and we run away from it. We say that writing down words to express ourselves is just not our thing, even though choosing not to write is no different than choosing not to speak. You can certainly give it a shot, but it's surely going to limit your ability to engage with the world around you. So why silence yourself? Why give in to fear and abandon this gift?

Simply, the practice of writing — having a documented conversation with yourself — is the key to understanding anything, so it's therefore understandable that it's something we overthink. In fact, I often encourage people to write things they normally wouldn't think to write as a way to better understand or

prepare. For example, I always encourage applicants of any job

to write out the interview before it happens. You can always

assume what questions will be asked, and you can simply make

up some more. Then, write your response. Actually write it

down. Write down the question, and your answer. Then build.

Add jokes. Add story structure. Add polish to sound more

professional. You don't have to memorize it, but the simple act

of writing it will make you more prepared than any other

candidate. By writing it, you understand it without overthinking

it, because if you leave it in your mind, it's sure to repeat on

itself, flip, spin, and disappear from inside your brain. It would

provide value to think about it, surely, but nowhere near what

you'd receive from writing it, because it would be documented

to allow you to develop and learn. I've offered that advice

countless times, and used it myself successfully, and yet no one

has ever reported back that they used it. It seems trivial, or

complicated, but that's just overthinking it.

Because writing is a collection of our thoughts, ideas, and feelings, all coming together with some desire or intended action, we believe that we *must* overthink it, that if it were so simple everyone would do it, that it has to be perfect, that this is the way it must be done. But, what you're forgetting is that writing *is* simple. The act of writing a job interview is incredibly simple, yet no one takes the advice. All you have to do is put the thoughts right there in your brain right there on the page, that's it, and your chances of success increases. Yet, we say we can't because writing is hard (it's not) or because our brains move too fast (they don't), but these are just excuses to explain away the fact that we're having difficulty putting our thoughts, ideas, and feelings onto the page where they can be discovered as incomplete, or flawed, or revealing. Stop, just stop, you're overthinking it.

The writing skill-set turns out to already be inside you, I promise. It's a fire inside that drives you to process, understand, create, and connect, and it's fueled by everything you've ever read, listened to, watched, and loved. But, sinking down on top of all of that, drowning it out, stifling the flames, is the fog of ego, anxiety, overconfidence, and self-doubt, preventing it from floating free as brilliant, crisp communication. If only you could find a way to unleash it; imagine what you'd write. Imagine what you'd craft if you felt capable and inspired. Imagine what you'd create when you felt uninhibited, confident, and free. Remember: you're imaginative, and playful, and have experienced many great, wonderful, memorable, sharable, things. In fact, your brain has memorized thousands upon thousands of words and is quite adept at stringing them up into sentences and launching them from your mouth without much thought. Just think about your last argument. Lots flew out there, huh? Maybe some shouldn't have. You were creating, but not editing. You were acting, not overthinking. You saw this rare, exciting, exhilarating mix of thought and passion. You were a Writer.

You're here now because you have recognized and imagined these things and yet your patterns and processes aren't working. You have all the necessary education and brain power to write effectively, and yet you still struggle — either to start, to finish, or both. This book will help you develop that simple, innate skill so you can become a better Writer, to set aside established patterns in order to look at things in a different way, to write as freely as if you were completely unbound by fear, self-consciousness, and clouds of thought.

As I've gotten older and placed in more managerial and directorial roles, my efforts are rarely about teaching someone how to write, but instead, teaching them how to get out of their own way to do something we're all not only already trained to do when we're children but that we're wired to do as human beings — tell stories, express, connect, communicate. Yet, all of my techniques, though helpful, are often turned aside at first as being too easy, too obvious, too simple, too dumb. It's only when I press on and they stumble still that they try them, and then they find that though thinking a little dumber and taking the sometimes obvious paths was the best writing process all along. So, onward we stagger together into something new, something entirely dumb, but absolutely worth not overlooking.

After many long years as a Writer, these are my dirty, dumb secrets. These techniques are what I find myself teaching every day. From TV shows to Fortune 500 boardrooms, I've found that writing is rarely an intellectual exercise, never perfect, and never without opposition. It's also certainly never an insurmountable feat. It's easier than everyone realizes, and anything can be accomplished with these tips and techniques designed to put words on page without excess thought or attachment. In fact, after all my years as a Writer, all of my advice can be summed up by the personal pursuit of just thinking less and always trying to be a bit dumber in my thoughts and actions.

And so, I welcome you to this stupid little book. Here, I'll teach you how to Write Dumb, to get out of your own way in order to stop overthinking the writing process so you can be a better, faster, more efficient, more creative Writer, because, quite simply, writing without thought is writing without worry, and we could all use a little less worry in our lives. I'll offer my methods for unleashing words onto the page with a wild fury. I'll share with you the dumbest tips and tricks imaginable, which will actually change the way you approach the written word from now on. Some are so dumb you might consider skipping them, but that would truly just be moronic, because they work, and this book is about dummifying and getting over yourself anyways — to simplify your thought processes, to judge less and write better, faster, every time — so it's time to get comfortable with being a dumb-dumb. When you do, even if just for a short few moments, your ability to shut off your inner critic and expert will help you realize your full potential as a fully-functioning creative Writer. So, here on out, this will be your guide to forgetting the fact that you're intelligent and educated. It'll be a simple methodology that helps you shake off the need to be perfect. It'll help you uncover that, deep down, you're already an exceptional Writer — you were just too dumb to notice.

Most likely, there's already a Writing for Dummies books, but that's not this book. I'm not smart enough to write one of those. Instead, I'm presupposing that as a Writer, or someone who wants to be a Writer, or just as someone who wants to write better, you're intelligent and driven and do not need things simplified to such a degree that I'd go so far as to actually call you a dummy. The point of this book is also certainly not to insult or degrade those with lesser intelligence, so if you want to get into an uproar about the use of words like 'idiot' or 'dumb' then good luck, because I welcome the free publicity. Shout it from the rooftops, you complete idiot! Tell everyone you know how horrible I am! Call your congressman! Don't forget social media, tell them too! Also, saying 'dumb' and 'moronic' and things like that will certainly not be the worst or most offensive things I say throughout this book, I promise. You've been warned.

Writing dumb is about abandoning ego, because writing itself is not about how smart we are, or how smart we think we are, or how educated we are, or how hardworking we are. It's simply about how good of a process we have, how simple and achievable it is, not how dynamic and impressive it is. It's about maintaining an approach to the words so as to stay ahead of them and not let them become those things we fear. Otherwise, you'll be overrun. You'll lose out to the endless possibilities that lie ahead. So, from this page forward, you're no longer intelligent, educated, and talented. You're a damn fool, free to explore and experiment with unknown, unexpected things without fear or ego. No one is looking over your shoulder. In fact, starting today, you're outside yourself. You're not even you. That's where you'll be free to discover that through it all, you were always an exceptional Writer standing in your own way, and now you're free to capitalize that W.

So, here we go. Forget what you learned in school, get ready to turn your normal brain functions off for a bit, and stop trying to show off with all your fancy words. Do not consider the future, the possibility, the critiques. Do not plan your success when you haven't even written a sentence. Simplify your thinking, calm your ego, strip away external forces, and write. Just write. But more importantly, stop overthinking it. They're just words, and none of us are perfict.

Alright, let's get dumb.

Let's Get Dumb

"One does not discover new lands without consenting

to lose sight of the shore for a very long time."

— Andre Gide

How stupid it is to even try to be a Writer. It's always against the

odds. It's never handed to you. And it's rarely a safe bet that

you'll be able to pay the bills long term. Like a soldier at war,

writing consists of long periods of soul-wrenching boredom

punctuated occasionally by brief moments of frenzied

excitement and absolute terror. And yet, so many of us actively,

joyfully pursue it. Hell, you're even reading this book to get

better at it, and I spent the time writing the damn thing! We're

fools running right toward that war, but at least we're in it

together.

The painful thing about all this, yet somehow the most

freeing thing, is that it's all on you, the individual, the Writer.

This is rarely a team effort, and therefore success, or lack of it, rests on your shoulders alone. Surely, I'm here to help, but this novel, this screenplay, this email to a customer, these words you hope to craft, whatever it is you're writing, it's all yours and yours alone, so everything hangs on your ability to reflect, and consider, and feel, and work, and perform — to always write more and think less. There's no one to blame, and there's no one to share the spotlight with. It's all on you, my foolish friend.

We're in for some shit, for sure, especially when you consider the environments in which we write and work. Regardless of our workplace or industry, we all operate in an achievement-oriented culture that celebrates our knowledge and accumulated skills, as well as our ability to display it or unleash it on demand. Admiration, and self-fulfillment, and all that stuff we crave, exist here. That's what makes it difficult to admit when we're ignorant or incapable, especially in terms of putting ideas on paper. Our average workplace environments are structured so that the subordinate does more asking, and the boss does more telling. It's considered general ignorance — but in the pursuit of understanding — to ask questions. Not only Writers but all of us try to exist in our problem-solving culture in which knowing things and being able to tell others, as opposed to asking others, is what's valued. And, those who "just get it" or who find ways to succeed without appearing ignorant are more commonly praised and promoted. So, our egos prevent us from asking questions — from revealing our ignorance or falling on our faces in failure and disgrace — because we're always in pursuit of success, and like how you have to dress for the job you want, you have to act the part, as well. And so we pretend that we know. We act like we can do anything. We fake it until we make it. Even if that means we do nothing, we learn nothing, we write nothing. But that is a sure-fire way to fail at life.

What makes writing dumb great is that it's all internal. It's in your head. It's private. In here, you're perfectly allowed to be an absolute dumb-dumb. You don't have to know things. You don't have to be right. You don't have to be perfect. No one's in here to be impressed. No one can see any of this. No one can hear these words bouncing around in your brain. No one can hear your inner voice reading yourself my words inside your head right now. It's all for you, and you alone, and in here, dumb is good. It means you're trying, and leaning, and advancing. Plus, admiration, and self-fulfillment, and all that stuff we crave, exist here, too. So, we begin in here, in your brain, and we feel free to fail in ridiculously dumb ways, and then we'll work outward from there.

For myself, my foolish journey toward self-fulfillment as a Writer ultimately began when I last met with my college advisor, who also happened to be the department head, and the professor of most of my classes. At that point, if anyone had an opinion on whether or not I had the ability to make a career of writing it was the woman who had read a majority of my work. Because of that, I was already doomed, but was too dumb to realize it.

What kind of Writer I wanted to be, I wasn't sure. Maybe TV or movies or novels or journalism or sports or whatever. I was unsure of everything except one thing: I wanted to write. I wanted my title to say "Writer." There was something romantic about that, something I could be proud of. But, when I posed this path as a possibility, as something that intrigued and interested me, she immediately shut me up. She pointed out the uncertainty, the strange hours, the lack of benefits, the competition, the talent required. She gave me no hope that I would, or even could, be a Writer. I don't remember how the rest of the meeting went, but what I do remember was walking out of her office. I was angry. And like any good creative, I tended to be "difficult." So, I did what any young, rebellious, "difficult" creative would do, I stole something from her. I grabbed a writing book off her shelf and walked out. Damn her, I would become a Writer, despite everything this expert had to say about it, and I would do so with her book as my guide. . I had done nothing impressive with words and showed no apparent aptitude, but I was both foolish enough and brave enough to do what I wanted. A good mix of those things and no one can stop you. Some want to write, some can't write, and some can't *not* write. What a gloriously dumb move I made that day because here we are...inside your brain...weird.

So, before we get into any writing, ever, let us first all humbly admit that we're idiots in some capacity, that this desire to be a Writer or to even try to express ourselves through these little symbols is foolish, and that every word we type will be a risk, but it will always be a risk worth taking. We must ignore those critics, no matter how accomplished, powerful, or knowledgeable they may be. We must follow the path we see fit for ourselves, even if there's no clear way through. We must agree that we do not know everything. It's not our brilliance that we should celebrate, but our awareness that we're not brilliant at all, because that self-awareness is something worthy of admiration, and self-fulfillment, and all that stuff we crave.

Dumb Writing Tip #1: Be dumb enough to believe.

Consider a room full of desks and people of all ages, genders, and ethnicities all silently writing around you. From their pens flow every idea, every point of view, every word. It's all there, in multitude. Whatever you want to write, someone else is already writing it in this very room. Out there in this sea of hard-working people are blog posts, screenplays, Broadway musicals, comic books, and crime novels. There are terrible ones and great ones, and everything in between. There are even boring old PowerPoint presentations, newsletters, student essays, and thank you cards to grandma. No matter the format or medium, everyone is writing and with so much out there, it all seems to be a race to find out who can their work out to the world the fastest.

So what's different about them? Why are they working so fast while you watch? Why does it seem so easy for them to keep their heads down and their words flowing? What sets them apart from you? What will ensure they finish when you don't? What makes them so special?

Answer: they don't realize they're in that room, let alone that it exists. What's holding you back from finishing your work and being a more efficient Writer is that you're quite aware of everyone around you. You're looking around while they focus. You're comparing yourself to everyone and everything. You're overthinking it all, and worrying too much, and drafting too much, and editing too much, making excuses instead of writing like everyone around you. It's not enough to just be in the room — to feel the energy of art being made, to say that you too are one of these special types. No, you have to contribute. Writing has never been a great spectator sport. You didn't come here to watch. You came to write.

So, your challenge is not merely to write, but to lose the basic realization that the world is full of Writers, that this world we live in is that very room. Yes, you are one in a great sea of minds, but to succeed, you will have to forget about it. You will have to put your head down and work. You will have to shut out the world, and you will have to shut off your anxious mind. You will have to stop thinking so damn much. And, you will have to do it without the everyday aid of reality TV, social media, and whatever else gives your brain a rest. You will have to embrace a mindful mindlessness that maintains your focus on the words and the words alone. You will have to pretend that you are the only Writer in this world, even for just a moment. You have to embrace opportunities to become a bit dumber to reality. It's the only way to write.

Dumb Writing Tip #2: Embrace your dumb.

Don't ever be afraid to be dumb, or to make mistakes, or to be the fool, or the outcast, or the one who stole from a university department head and were probably on camera during the whole stupid, worthless crime, even if that stolen book has served as a relic and trophy of personal success for almost twenty years. But, most especially, don't be afraid to be dumb in the things you do for yourself, as yourself, inside your own brain, where you're free from judgement, critique, attack, and all that negative stuff.

Admit you don't know things and chase after knowledge and ability at every opportunity. Grow in all the good ways. Have the audacity to go after your goals with everything you've got; chase after them with a stick! You'll be much happier when you do. And, you must never get to the point where your confidence prevents you from doing the simple things in life and in work. As soon as you get to the point where you think, "I've got this. I've mastered this," that's when you start cutting corners. That's when you actually make dumb mistakes that ruin your writing. That's when you stop exploring new ways of working. Even when writing a simple thank you letter to your department head for their advice, where you mention borrowing a book, but only because you thought you might have maybe remembered noticing a camera after you already stole it, you must consider that smart writing requires you to be dumb first. You must stay true to a process. You must be open to making mistakes in your head and on the page. You must be comfortable taking steps, not leaps, and doing so every single time. The moment you think you can no longer fail is when you fail most miserably. But, when you know you can fail, and you also know it's worth it to try, that's when you're sure to succeed.

The Heart & The Head

"Creativity involves breaking out of established patterns

in order to look at things in a different way."

- Edward de Bono

Alright, let's get into some real dumb advice by simplifying all

writing, no matter the medium, into just two basic parts.

All writing is crafted into existence based on two things,

and two things only. If you can understand these two things, and

utilize them correctly, you can write anything — faster and

further. I've used these two things as a way to express specific

"mindsets" in order to focus my Writer's brain and emotions

toward the right target in the right way, at the right time. It's a

process designed to help the Writer exist as individual personas,

or different parts of one's self, with the personas reflecting the

different mindsets needed to not only write effectively across

mediums but to add depth to any writing project. Simply, it's to

become two completely different Writers. Now, don't over-

complicate it in your mind — don't overthink it. It's much

simpler than it seems. You, as a Writer, are already made up of two halves. One is the Heart, and the other is the Head. One side is filled with emotion and energy. The other is based on, and delivers, sheer logic. One feels, the other thinks. Each excels at specific writing tasks, so they're yours to call upon when needed.

Heart writing is the writing that you can't plan or schedule. It's the emotional stuff that sneaks up on you like song lyrics while you're driving, or a brilliant movie concept while drinking with friends, or like a poem in the middle of the night. It's the writing that happens entirely by accident when you weren't thinking all that much. It's chaotic and magical. Meanwhile, Writing with Head is something planned. It's the exact number of pages you say you'll do tomorrow at 6 AM, at your desk, with a hot coffee, and a shawl sweater, but not if one of those things is altered in any way. It's about control and structure.

The great secret to writing is to not accept that structure, and form, and writing styles are concrete and unbreakable —

that you can only write certain things at certain times in certain ways, or through outline. Nor is it to accept that words are something you wait for — magic floating in the air, gifted to you from the gods. The trick is not to be or harness one or the other — it's to be and harness both. To conquer all types of writing at any time, day or night, at home or at work, is to simply use some really dumb techniques that teach you how to turn on the two sides of your writing brain so you can write what you want, what you need, whenever without feeling like you're making an overt, complicated effort.

Without overthinking it, the Heart and the Head can be envisioned as two parts of one whole, like the Chinese principal of yin and yang. They're seemingly opposite forces, each representing something individual and specific, yet they work together to create something greater — something powerful and Earth-moving — while also showing glimpses of one another in themselves. Believe it or not, in every great rom-com Writer, there's a careful, logical strategist who adores the structure of their screenplays. In every great Writer of high school textbooks, there's a poet who writes only in unrelenting passion and emotion. Your Heart and Head are a symbiotic flow of thought, feeling, and all-around energy that you can harness to write. Together, it's a great, natural, unstoppable power, and it's already inside you, just waiting to be recognized and let loose.

These two sides of your Writer's self are order and chaos, with Head being order and Heart being chaos. It's a symbiotic, cyclical relationship, with one always leading to the other. Because, as a creative, when you have order, you want to create chaos, and when you have chaos, you want to create order. However, there is a time and place for each to exist and operate, and so when you must write there, you must stay there, avoiding temptation from the other. When you have one, the other seems appealing, comfortable, intriguing, and sexy. The question becomes, when to use which side of your Writer's mind?

Consider your Heart and Head a rotating effort of chaos and control. One feeds the other and they continuously flow onward, coiling round and round. When chaos and imagination aren't working for you, add control, and structure, and routine.

When control leaves you stuck, incorporate chaos into it to

spark new ideas, breaking you lose so you're free to explore

what's possible.

Oftentimes, when too much time is spent with order,

you need chaos to spark further creativity. With too much

chaos, you need order to actually create something digestible

and understandable. When you begin with chaos, you create

wildly, crafting more and more thoughts, ideas, and perspectives.

When you follow that with order, you can structure it, cutting it

down and forming it into something valuable. But, if you lead

with order, you have nothing to build with. And, if you end with

chaos, you end up never finishing, because there's always more

more more ideas to pack in and you can't stop long enough to

figure out where it goes and how.

As every one of us humans naturally possess these two

parts within ourselves, each of us also has a dominant side,

reflected in our different writing styles, preferred mediums, and

processes. You're either predominantly Heart or predominantly

Head. This is why writing poetry appeals more to some (The Hearts) and writing historical novels based on heavy research appeals more to others (The Heads). Various inputs and influences can determine a shift from one to the other, but commonly, we lean toward one specifically.

When writing, there's always a time for the logic of the Head and approaching your work carefully. Then there's a time for you to unleash raw emotion with absolute Heart. In anything you write, you must apply both but at different stages of your writing process. While particular writing projects — from a simple company email to a blockbuster movie — require either the Heart or the Head to be more dominant in the work, anything good utilizes both by moving back and forth between the two halves as needed. By recognizing these two parts of yourself — the Heart and the Head — you can call upon one and then the other to write more simply, not overthinking or over-feeling. For example, too often, when trying to write something emotional — something that a reader can connect with — we're thinking strategically and logically, as in, "What will compel this reader to want to read this?" Or, "What will convert this

audience to buy, or act?" In these moments, what we need to do

is think less and feel more — utilizing the Heart, not the Head.

We need to let the words and feelings flow naturally. We need

to connect to the emotions of the reader through actual feeling,

not through analysis. We cannot think our way to emotional

connections, just as we cannot feel our way to logic and

rationale. So, to get to our goals, we need to utilize the correct

part of our Writer's self at the correct time, utilizing both

through our journey. We need to not just write a song but write

one that's both emotionally powerful and structurally sound.

That's something that's truly worth singing about.

Utilizing both aspects of your mind and soul simply

requires you to recognize that they exist. You're neither a robot

that is entirely logic and process, nor are you entirely Heart; a

Disney princess, made only of curiosity, emotion, and

imagination. You're both of these and all of it, all jammed up

into one. Your recognition of them, and your ability to already

access them whether you realize it or not, is what makes you more adept at being a Writer than others. Your knowledge and feeling that they're inside of you is what brought you here to learn more about letting them out onto the page when you need them most.

Unless you're writing something that needs it, like a poem filled with raw emotion or a technical document with raw fact and nothing else, you'll want to merge the two parts of your writing and thinking into one complete whole. After-all, as you carry your reader through your words, like a story, you'll need rising and falling emotions and thoughts over a period of time. You'll need to use the two parts to push and pull them where you want them to go, pulling the right lever at the right time to hold and guide their interest. Too flowery and emotional and they may become repulsed. Too cold, corporate, and robotic, and they will become bored.

However, finding those precise moments when to use Heart of Head takes time, practice, luck, and confidence. There is no right answer or formula, or someone would have made a lot of money off of it consistently. Every great writer wrote garbage, so even the greats clearly don't know the precise notes of emotion and logic, and when to play them exactly. Instead, I recommend thinking higher level with these two parts of your writer's brain. Don't think of the small moments, but the entire writing process by employing one and then the other in your journey. One, and then the other, that's it. First find inspiration and possibility with Heart, and then structure it with Head. Consider every idea and feeling you can muster, and then consider them all, forming and reforming through thought and logic. Heart, then Head. Give yourself time to play with words without limitations, and then follow that up with time of absolute limitations — time, structure, and focus.

Business leader, UX designer, and writer Mona Patel wrote a children's book called *The Thing About Swings*, which is actually quite relevant for Writers of any age. This is a book that's disguised as a children's book but is really about decision making and innovation for adults, "inspiring children of all ages to question, dream, and design a better world." In it, the elephant thinks up a million ideas, always asking "What if?" but never doing anything about it. That elephant is all Heart — full of wonder, passion, and possibility. Contrary to that elephant is the skunk, who challenges every idea. "We don't have the budget. We don't have the time," the skunk always responds. The skunk is the Head of the group. It cares only about *how* things will be done, and wants a plan that controls and binds the idea. If the skunk doesn't have it, then it's not a good idea, because it's not clear and logical. It can't imagine a way forward for the idea, while the elephant doesn't care to think about such menial things like plans, process, or limitations of space and time. Meanwhile, the orangutan stops dreaming and challenging and simply gets to work. There's a time to be the elephant and lead with curiosity, wonder, and Heart. There's a time to be the skunk, to slow things down, to use logic, to use your Head. And, there's a time to be the orangutan, to be practical and imaginative, to apply both curiosity and logic, Heart & Head, but more important, to stop talking and just get things done — to just shut up and work. This is your effort — to not merely be a Heart or a Head, but to be both, and to stop thinking and ideating so much and just get to work.

Understanding the Heart

Diving deeper into these two parts of your Writer's self, the Heart, the Feeler, likes to experience the emotion of the project more. It tends to be more frantic and "all over the place," and is less strategic, capable, or interested in developing a plan prior to "creating."

Your Heart is also more romantic and driven by the ability to use their imagination and bring new, never-before-seen things to life. It thrives on diving in head first for some play time, and it's far more comfortable with trial and error than the Head. When faced with a challenge, it drives the Writer to be more open to seeking out information themselves. It sees that not having new ideas quickly, a lack of focus, and a feeling of being redundant as challenges, and portraying a lack of humanity as its greatest fear.

The Heart is easily distracted, which it only uses as an excuse to not write, especially when there are so many more possibilities to consider. In this endless brainstorm, everything is further research and useful, and therefore nothing ever gets done. The Heart is like a small child that's distracted and mesmerized by the world around it, observing everything with wonder and curiosity. With this mindset, waiting for inspiration is an excuse not to write, and searching for inspiration is also an excuse not to write. That's why focus and controlled output from the little bit of Head in this yin yang relationship within you are required to get the Heart to do any work.

The Hearts of the writing world are freewheeling and erratic, better being able to ideate and expand on thinking quickly. They're known for creating new worlds, wonder, exploration, and possibility, not for formulas or reboots. To see someone writing with Heart is to see someone in love with words and ideas. It's like a singer closing their eyes as they sing. Sometimes it can be annoying, but when it's good, it's damn good.

Freewriting, brainwriting, or flow of consciousness writing is a useful tool for letting your Heart speak without thought or inhibitions clouding it, because being "all over the place" is the very nature of that style of writing. There is no form, no structure, no purpose, no deadline — just a natural flow that's connected to some part of you usually hidden and restricted by self-conscious. The trick is to shut the world off, to not think, even for a few moments, in order to let yourself slip into a flow state where ideas flow naturally. And, most importantly, you must never, ever try to be perfect. Give yourself time to create, and know that it will likely be useless, because it very likely will be, and that is okay — this is all part of the process. Hold yourself to no standards, because if you do, you will never meet them.

Shutting off your inner critic and your need for a structured deliverable, on a structured timeline, is quite difficult for Heady writers. It will never be easy on your first, second, or possibly even the twentieth time, but simply put your pen to the paper, or whatever medium serves you best, and write without thinking. Just know your Heart is there, let your feelings flow, and see where they take you.

Understanding the Head

The Head, or the Thinker, likes to be more structured in the writing approach. It likes a process that defines how and when the work will be done, as well as a clear objective for how the work will be created, and then how it will exist throughout and following the journey. It likes a certain, trusted path to walk down based on experience. Trial and error is only achievable once this path has been thoroughly followed. This includes following writing schedules, a specific structure based on the project, a clear outline, and a firm, unbreakable deadline. It likes you to sit in the same chair to write, at the same time of day, with the same coffee. It sees maintaining self-confidence, as well as understanding itself and the reader, as challenges, and sounding too "ooey-gooey emotional" as its greatest fear, because it worries about coming across as vulnerable.

Despite its flaws, the Thinkers are purposeful and precise, better being able to hit a target from afar. As a Thinker, you know, can predict, and can explain things clearly and purposefully with great detail. When activated, the Thinker likes to be in charge and to be present, aware of everything. It's like an old man giving you perfect directions, because he remembers the good old days before GPS, and he therefore knows every landmark and turn along the way.

To elevate or call upon the Head, whether because you prefer it or find it most difficult to utilize, give yourself structure and never break it, ever. Choose a small writing project and give yourself guidelines, a timeline, rules, and order, and then follow that path. Create a writing space and tell yourself exactly what you will write there and by when, and say it out loud to confirm it. Sit down and follow your plan perfectly, step by step, literally focusing on only one thing at a time.

As you write, the Heart inside you will want to play with everything and will quickly become bored with focusing so much on one little thing at a time. It will want to explore what happens next, and it will want to reference a song you kinda remember, or it will want to go Google that weird thing you kinda remember from when you were a kid, and it will want to be more, and do more. And in that moment, you will see that your Head is all that keeps you on track. It's why people have movie ideas but have never finished a screenplay — they write with all Heart and not enough Head. They lack structure and order in their writing; not necessarily *in* their screenplay, but in the act of writing it.

Meanwhile, the Head can lead you to suffer from anxiety and depression and a lack of confidence due to its tendency to overthink, to be overly practical, and to form cognitive distortions. For example, "If I write this, people will see me, and if they see me they will judge me, and if they judge me I will fail. Then I won't have a job, or money, or friends, so that's why I should just not write it, or anything, ever." Or, it considers the possibility of a career, or lack thereof, as a Writer in most industries and says, "Why bother? It's not likely to happen anyway." So, while the Heart can be a woo-woo weirdo, the Head can be a real drag.

Your 3 Rooms

Legend has it that the incomparable innovator Walt Disney used a similar thinking technique to the Heart and the Head as the creative process for himself, as well as his animation teams. It was called Disney's Three Rooms.

Both inside our heads as well as actual physical manifestations in their office, the Three Rooms helped you focus your mind at a given time and then more effectively and efficiently turn your dreams into reality. These Three Rooms were said to have reflected the three Walts. There was the Dreamer, the Realist, and the Critic, and you never knew which Walt would be joining you.

Much like the Heart, the Dreamer allowed for absolute creativity and imagination. It was where the work began and where ideas flourished. This was not a room for negativity, or opposition, or critique. There was no place for all that when everyone's minds and hearts were wide open, always considering the possibility of new and wonderful things. Here, anything was possible, and that's why it gave animators the freedom to craft experiences and stories that would change the world.

Similar to the Head, the Realist brought structure and deep, mindful, logical consideration into the work now that it existed. While the Dreamer was fueled by divergent thinking with the mind focused on the many possible considerations and possibilities, the Realist transforms the thinking by embracing convergent thinking to the creation process. In this mindset, and sometimes physical location, risk-taking and originality are replaced by data, experience, and logic. Here, we can take wild, free, fun ideas and edit them into a structure or form that is practical and achievable. Simply, this is where order is given to ideas. (Heart, and then Head)

The Critic is the final and most annoying room. This is where we have to be honest with ourselves, each other, and the work, and where we sometimes have to kill our babies, as in getting rid of the ideas that we do so dearly love, but which we know will not succeed. This is the time when logic still reigns supreme but emotion is still incredibly important. It's not simply, "This will not work." It's also strongly, "This will not resonate with people." In this room we'll decide if this Disney animation is truly what will make the kiddos of the world dance and sing, and at times cry. Or, if it's just doomed to fail.

And, like the Heart and the Head making a greater whole, each of these three creative mindsets must work alongside another "room" at some point or they become ineffective. For example, the work created by the Dreamer will often be unstructured and unachievable without the Realist. It will be only pixie dust; fantasy and therefore not practical. But, by incorporating the Realist, the wonderful ideas crafted by the Dreamer can be molded into something incredible and valuable — something worth sharing. However, while the Dreamer and the Realist make a great team, the Dreamer and Critic would only fight, and the Realist and the Critic would have very little to work with without the Dreamer's ideas. That's why the foundation of the Dreamer and Realist, or the Heart and the Head, are critical to the creative process.

In addition to providing an ever-shifting mindset for you, the Writer, the Heart and the Head can also be your step-by-step process, much like Disney's physical rooms. The subsequent sections of this book will introduce more extremely dumb tips & techniques for utilizing these two halves of yourself as an approach to tackling any writing project by being one and then the other. In this approach, the Heart will allow you to write freely and openly — a Dreamer and wild brainstormer that helps you prepare yourself with words and ideas. Then, the Head will help you create structure, balance intent, and be a Realist. In two simple steps, you stop constantly trying to write or create in your head, and you just take a backseat to things within you that already exist by merely recognizing their existence and specific, timely role.

Finally, once you've taken the two steps, these two halves and their dumb tips & tricks will work together to create a self-critic — much like the third room — that will allow you to properly review your work once it's actually done, and not

before as you try to write it. It's the Heart + the Head = the

Human. So, as you dive into your next bit of writing, no matter

what it is, work from the Heart and the Head, and appeal to the

human on the other side.

Dumb Writing Tip #3: Use your Heart and your Head.

Use both your emotions and your logic, not just one or the

other. Consider what the reader wants, and then what they need,

or vice versa. Ask yourself what would be amazing, and then

what is practical. If one way isn't working, try using the other.

Never follow the simple, yet common, advice of Writers

to merely open a vein and bleed. Surely, to write with Blood is a

major part of writing. It is in fact pure Heart. But, that is not

enough. To actually write successfully, one must embrace not

just their raw passion but also their structured mind — both the

Heart and the Head, together. You can't just open a vein and bleed, you must then do something with the Blood. You have to put it to work and translate it for the reader.

Another way to think about it: Think of the Heart as a chef. They're artists and while they do use recipes, they'll also improvise with what they have. They follow their senses and try new things — a bit more spice here, a splash of salt there. They're one with the kitchen — connected to it in a way that can't be explained. They explore the space, open their hearts, take inspiration from the natural world, and let the food guide them, not the recipe.

Meanwhile, a baker is the Head. The recipe must be followed because the product is more susceptible to failure without the precise structure it provides. A loaf of bread or a cupcake only have so much room for variance. Certainly, the baker can apply some Heart — some inspired creativity — but at its core, the baker is guided by structure, not freedom of the moment. But, together, the mindset of the chef and baker can create magical, memorable meals.

When you use them both as you write, structure, and edit, the combined self, the Human, full of both emotion and logic, will better critique and review your work. This will free you from cold, corporate, robotic language, and it will ground your emotional, dreamy, imaginative ideas. You will be more readable for all, while also being more targeted for your specific audience.

When instructing writers on writing with Heart, I have them break their writing time in half. The first part is theirs to explore, to feel out the project. The second half is mine, in that they have that amount of time to actually get the work done for me. However, the two cannot clearly overlap — they cannot and should not start writing during the first block of time. They must ignore that fast-approaching deadline and instead trust in themselves that the work will get done eventually. They must give themselves the time to explore, and just stop thinking so much. I recommend listening to music that reminds them of the work, or going for walks. I pull quotes that are similar in nature, and talk a lot about what the writing could look like later. This time is merely for finding the Heart of the project, and

connecting to it in some emotional way, but not actually doing

any writing. They have to feel it, not plan it. Head-driven writers

find this exploration time to be wasteful and scary. But,

regardless if you're a Heart or a Head, what I find is that when

they accomplish the first part, the second comes more easily

than they could have ever imagined. If they spent the first

amount of time feeling the work more, they no longer have to

think. Somehow, they know exactly what to write, as if the words

are flowing straight through them from somewhere else —

somewhere magical, maybe.

Getting Started

"The thing is to become a master and in your old age

to acquire the courage to do what children did

when they knew nothing."

- Ernest Hemingway

Before we can write anything, we first need ideas. We need

something to write about, and we have to think it all up using

our imagination. Now, we've all seen the countless Medium

articles and LinkedIn posts about how creative we all were as

kids, that we only grew up and out of our imagination. Kids

leverage vast stores of imagination, but as adults, our day-to-day

lives force us to focus more on the logical and practical nature of

life, and less so on our imaginations. Whether our imagination

goes away or we simply don't leverage it anymore, like an

atrophied muscle, it withers. But, creativity is not just

imagination. That's only one part of it. The other part is

knowledge, practicality, and experience, which is driven by the Head. Yes, there truly is a practical side to creativity. That's how we make it actionable. That's how we put it to work. That's how we achieve and craft something imaginative but believable — a journey people can take, not just consider.

As a Writer, you can utilize inspiration from the world around you and inside yourself and then funnel it, transform it, into something entirely new—something that will inspire emotion, change, and action. The process of purposefully getting there directly, as opposed to waiting for it, is ideation. When ideating, or brainstorming, as well as when writing, you must use both the Heart and the Head. What is logical and what is wonderful? What is the possible and what is the impossible? Your ability to weigh them, to balance them, is what will differentiate your work from others. Shift too far one way and your work is too cold and robotic. Shift too far the other and it's unbelievable and chaotic. Find a comfortable spot in the middle and that's the Goldilocks sweet spot all Writers dream of.

Logical thinking is the Head, and imagination is the

Heart. A kid, while imaginative, is not a good problem solver.

They do not yet possess the functional aspects of creativity.

They're raw, pure, unadulterated Heart. Too often we grow up

and become too much Head — too logical, not enough passion,

emotion, carelessness. We fail to take chances. We fail to fail.

However, without proper and complete brainstorming that

considers them both, any writing effort will suffer. To write

anything worthy of your time, you have to spend some time

thinking about it, letting it grow and take shape. Want to write a

novel? You must find your big idea before you can start writing

it. Same goes for blog articles, or movies, or love letters.

Brainstorming is just coming up with the ideas that will populate,

guide, and fuel your writing. But, as serious and vital as

brainstorming is to your writing, it still requires you be a bit

childish. That means, no matter your age, no matter your job

title, no matter how serious and professional you think you are,

for you to write even a good text, you're going to have to open

up your heart a bit. Be imaginative, be passionate, be excited, be vulnerable, and then put it down for the logic to mold it, but never before. Ideas come through imagination, and then are bettered through logic and consideration — The Heart then the Head.

So, it's time to start coming up with ideas, whether it's to determine what you're going to write or what will make up what you're writing. Ideas can be anything that guides and populates your writing. This time before you actually write is the time in which you open yourself up to thinking, not when you try to limit it. And remember, great ideas come from some pretty dumb places, so this should be some fun.

Brainstorming Tips

"Creativity is inventing, experimenting, growing, taking risks, breaking rules, making mistakes, and having fun."

- Mary Lou Cook

Dumb Brainstorming Tip #1: Do your research.

Know your goals. Know your boundaries. Know your brand.
Know your competition. Know what they're doing. Know what's
cool. Know what's winning awards. Know what's emerging.
Know what success looks like. All of this means fully
comprehending what you're doing — what you're writing and
why — and then spending a good amount of time online studying
awards sites, blogs, and competitors' social pages. The more you
uncover, the more you have to work with. Brainstorming
without this context is worthless. Your research fuels you for
your writing, and it contains you. The "think outside the box"
mantra is garbage. You want the box. You need the box. You
love the box. It allows you to stay focused on what you're writing
so you can know all these things that are valuable to making it a
success without getting carried away in unworthy ideas.

Dumb Brainstorming Tip #2: Go down the rabbit hole.

Even though you want to stay focused with your research, that does not mean unexpected things can't inspire you. Music, art, anime, whatever; let anything and everything light your creative fire inside you. Cherish Google search, look at similar categories, look at entirely different categories, look at language and imagery, look at anything and everything. Good ideas come from good ideas, so let others inspire you, no matter where you find it. If you're writing a blog article, read every other article you can find on the same subject, and copy & paste the good stuff into a document to use later, remembering to color-code so as not to plagiarize. If you're writing advertisements for a luxury brand, search other luxury brands, and not just what words they use. Note the sentence lengths and their punctuation. Don't just copy & paste the words, take the whole ad. Let it visually inspire you throughout the time you spend writing. If it inspires you now, you might need it to inspire you again later, and you won't want to have to go search for it again.

When writing TV and radio advertisements for Mercedes-Benz, I would need to quickly and completely come up with, and write, ideas around the luxury living you could find in a Mercedes automobile. The challenge was that I was in no way living a luxurious life. I was a young copywriter, so luxury for me was not drinking **PBR** after work and instead upgrading to a luxurious Bud Light. So, to get into the mindset, I would not only watch and listen to old Mercedes ads, I would review their competitors' ads. I'd study what they were saying and doing, and then consider what they weren't saying and doing. If they were doing that, what could I do to make my brand sound better, more luxurious in comparison? I also wouldn't bind myself to TV and radio alone. I'd scroll through Google Images for other luxury items. Rolex watches. High fashion brands. Fancy airlines. The most expensive mattresses. Everything I found created a luxurious mindset in which I could later write more effectively. They gave me a list of words, headlines, and taglines to use as a foundation. They showed me what everyone else was doing so I knew what not to do, and what not to say. In a few hours of scrolling, I was becoming a bit of an expert in the field, and could talk about it in great detail later with the client.

The simple act of exploring and going down a rabbit hole gave me the understanding and boundaries I needed to create something I otherwise might not have understood.

Dumb Brainstorming Tip #3: Give yourself time.

Good ideas come after they've had a chance to bounce around in your subconscious for a while. Take small moments whenever possible to just let it all sink in. Think about it while you drive, or play a mindless video game on mute while recording yourself talking. Take a walk, take a shower, take a long poop even! Look for opportunities to go into a mental flow state while ideating where time and space seem to disappear. Look to disconnect and look at things differently. This usually happens outside of 9 to 5 work hours. Sorry. It's not always convenient to you. Ideas will sneak up on you, and surprise you, if you let them. But, that's where the best ideas come from. They show up in the middle of the night and make you write them down, or they'll go away, never to come back. Take those ideas seriously, because you are on their time, not yours, and if you don't respect them, they'll fly off to the next person.

Dumb Brainstorming Tip #4: Question everything.

If you don't know what to ask, start with journalistic questions: who, what, when, where, and why? Write yourself a series of questions and answers like you're interviewing yourself, and actually answer the questions as if someone else asked them. It allows you to break away from feeling normal and access different parts of your brain. It makes the problems and challenges clear, so you can start solving for them in creative ways. Just be sure to write these questions and answers down or you are sure to lose them in your mind.

Dumb Brainstorming Tip #5: Make connections.

As Steve Jobs once said, creativity is just connecting things. When you ask creative people how they did something, they feel a little guilty because they didn't really do it—they just saw an obvious opportunity to make something, to take a chance, to

take leaps others didn't know were possible. Creativity, at its

core, is really just pattern recognition. It's combining disparate

things to reveal something new. You goal is simply to make

connections that can inspire new thinking. To get there, you

have to look at the world around you. Look at your ideas. Study

them, consider them. This is one of the hardest things to do for

people who don't own their creativity because it takes time and

the ability to turn off your inner self critic as you make weird and

wonderful connections in the world.

Dumb Brainstorming Tip #6: Make buckets.

As part of filtering your thinking, as well as managing the stored-

up information you've uncovered, try thinking in buckets.

Different buckets should represent different things, so your

ideas exist in diverse categories. Brand pillars, content pillars,

story acts, chapters — these can all be associated with buckets.

Try coming up with a few ideas and then matching them up into

common threads. Those threads are your buckets, so just start dropping ideas in. If ideas overlap buckets, they might be too

complex or unclear. If the buckets are empty, you're probably

not done ideating. When they're full, simplify, even as far as

single words. For example, "This is my emotional idea, this is

my inspirational idea, and this is my aspirational idea."

Dumb Brainstorming Tip #7: Flip it on its head.

Challenge everything. If it's a holiday-themed ideation for a

scene or a brand promotion or even a Christmas card,

reconsider what you know. If everyone thinks the holidays are

happy, what if they're actually stressful for your reader? What if

people don't want to cook for family, but instead they really just

want to escape and not think of recipes at all and they want you

to talk about, because then they won't feel alone, or weird, or

Grinchy? Coming up with ideas can sometimes be inspired by

coming up with the exact opposite of what you're supposed to

be thinking about. If it's, "How can we come up with the world's

most comfortable mattress?" Instead try, "What is everything I

hate about mattresses?" This alternative thinking often leads you to new thinking by taking an unexpected path to the idea. Flip things on their head, look at them differently, and accept nothing as fact or gospel. Allow both the Head and the Heart chances at ideating and providing a point of view.

Dumb Brainstorming Tip #8: Talk it out.

Your singular mindset will always be limited. It's only one point of view, even with the dual Heart and Head concept. You've lived one life, and have one very specific way of thinking, writing, and ideating. That's why it's extremely powerful to get outside your own head, not just to get a new mindset but also to allow yourself the chance to process your ideas in a different way. So, take someone for a walk and explain your thinking. Say it all out loud. Give them everything. In fact, explain it to them like they're an idiot so you don't leave anything out, only trying to sound great by giving them the juicy stuff. Give them the opportunity to help you grow your ideas. Let them ask questions and poke holes in things. This is not a time to impress. This is a time to be dumb, to share your dumb ideas, and to not allow your ego or sensitivity prevent ideas from living and growing.

Dumb Brainstorming Tip #9: First idea, worst idea.

Never settle. If it was your first idea, it was everyone's first idea. This can mean it's basic and needs to die, or it can be so good and right that everyone got there for a reason. When you share it, like in the previous tip, and everyone loves it, consider it. But, otherwise, keep ideating. Your first idea is just the beginning. If ideating were easy, you wouldn't need tips and tricks for it. It's outside our everyday way of living. It's complicated. But, it's also quite fun, if you let it, so get to idea two, then three, and keep going. You have to put in the effort. You'll find that it's an amazing thing in that you can predict how little effort most people are going to put into their work. From Writers to their readers, we're all tapped for time, and looking for shortcuts. That's why in order to get to the big, great, memorable ideas — the ones that make people forget about time altogether — you have to abandon your first ideas. Assume your competition is settling, but never yourself settle.

I began this practice of never stopping at my first idea not through writing but through art. In college art classes, when a project was given to the class, I would recognize the first big idea that came to my brain, and then immediately abandon it, because I knew others would have the same idea, and then every project looked the same and I wanted to stand out. For example, back in the early 2000s, a hate crime was perpetrated on my college campus. In response, our professor tasked us with using the remains of equal rights books that were destroyed during the crime as papier mache to create pieces that reflected the pain that members of the LBGTQ community faced every day. If the books were destroyed in hate, they would find new life in love and support. It was a great project, but I knew what everyone was going to do, because it was my first thought, as well. We were still experiencing the aftermath of the Matthew Shepard case from a few years before, in which he was brutally tortured and beaten, and left to die on a fence in Wyoming. I knew immediately that the professor was about to see 30+ papier mache fences, because it was an obvious idea, and people are

lazy. So I made something else. At the following class, there

were 30+ fences and one weird thing I made. Was mine good?

Hahaha, no, definitely not. I was, and to this day remain, a

terrible artist. But, I got an A, because mine stood out. The

professor enjoyed and appreciated mine more because it was

not everything else she was seeing and experiencing. The same

can be said about movies, books, blog content, social posts,

emails from a vendor — anything someone will read and

experience in their daily lives. And, only now after all these years

do I see the symbolism of the fences figuratively holding

everyone in creatively and artistically. Yay, writing!

Dumb Brainstorming Tip #10: Get weird.

The comfort zone is the great enemy to creativity. Weird

inspires. It brings energy to the moment, it makes the process of

writing and ideating fun. So, put the weirdest, most out-there

thing you can think of on paper, and be comfortable doing so.

Let the imaginative Heart speak up for a moment. (Like, using human hair from barber shops inside coats for recycled warmth

and limiting the use of down! No, you're weird.) Feel free to not

just step but LEAP out of yourself and your comfort zone to

spark creative thinking. Never stick to routines or you'll come

up with routine ideas. (Now, if you'll excuse me, I'm expecting a

call from Patagonia about my brilliant hairy jackets idea.)

Dumb Brainstorming Tip #11: Keep your ideas simple.

As legendary SCAD advertising professor Luke Sullivan says,

"Your idea should fit on a Post-It Note." Great ideas are

complex but seem simple. Bad ideas are often simple but seem

complex. If it's hard to explain now, it will be impossible to

explain to someone else, so keep it simple. Write it short and

make it sticky. (FREE human hair + jacket = affordable,

sustainable warmth!)

Don't force complexity into ideas or stories. Allow them

to exist as simply as possible. By doing so, you not only make it

easier to understand, you allow yourself to see it as achievable.

Complex ideas are daunting. And, people get bored listening to them. Your fearful, anxious, practical human side will come out to whisper in your ear how little time you have to dedicate to ravelling and unravelling this beast of an idea. Shut that jerk down by tricking it into thinking your idea is so simple that it would be foolish not to see it through to the end!

Dumb Brainstorming Tip #12: Drink, don't think.

A beer can help stimulate your creativity, and it helps you relax while you come up with bunches of ideas. And, a bourbon works harder than a beer. Trust me, it's science! The more relaxed you are, the less self-conscious you are, and the fun will flow in the form of ideas worth writing. Whether you're in a group or riding solo, fun, happy, relaxed brainstorming is good brainstorming. When you loosen up, ideas flow, and everything seems like a good idea. Good ideas inspire more good ideas, but remember that the time to edit comes later. Don't kill an idea before it has a chance to live and grow. Later, when you're done with your bourbon-fueled ideas, swap the booze for a coffee so you can focus and edit out things that were just too damn weird for the world, like putting human hair inside a Patagonia jacket. Christ, who came up with the dumb-dumb idea?

Dumb Brainstorming Tip #13: Pretend you're high.

You could just get high, but here's a low-cost shortcut: By pretending to be high, you abandon yourself and let your unrestrained self come through. Ask yourself, "How would this look & sound if I were high? Would it be funny? What colors would it sound like? How would my body respond? Is hair growing out of my face?!? Why am I walking weird? Wait, I'm not walking, I'm sitting and the room is walking!!!!" By pretending your brain is chemically altered, your brain is actually slightly, yet safely, altered and so will your way of thinking. At the very least, it will be fun, and the creative juices will take over.

Dumb Brainstorming Tip #14: Be a kid.

Act like a curious child and view the world with wonder and amazement. Take a quick walk outside and look at the clouds like you did when you were little. Play with acorns. Talk in funny voices. Write with your opposite hand. Write a poem in crayon. Even a simple use of rhyming or alliteration that you otherwise would have never paid any attention to can be astonishing if viewed the right way, especially when written in crayon. Anything really can be seen as awesome and more memorable when viewed through the eyes of a child. Like, type some words real quick on your laptop. Watch the blinking line turn into letters, like really fast. It's awesome, isn't it? I just wrote that! And that, too! The world's a wonderful place, if you let it be. And, this shift in perspective allows you to abandon your adult experiences in which you may have become cynical of work, and writing, and critics, and clients, and everything else.

Dumb Brainstorming Tip #15: Take off your headphones.

Writers became stunted in the early 2000s. That's because we were introduced to those little white earbuds in the iPod, and later the iPhone. They became so commonplace that walking out of your home without them felt uncomfortable. City

sidewalks were covered with people subtlety blocking out the

world with Apple earbuds, and the result is that we stopped

listening to the world around us. We ended up becoming one

dimensional in our writing, because we lost a valuable channel of

content flowing into our ears throughout our daily lives. So,

surround yourself with people and their noise, like at a bar or

cafe, and listen to not just what they say, but how they say it.

Listen for emotion, conflict, strife, slang, personality. Discover

new ways of viewing the world. This will help your escape your

point of view, and will diversify your way of thinking to match

with people you passively encounter.

Dumb Brainstorming Tip #16: Get moving.

It's an absolute myth that writing happens in a stationary

position. Writing requires energy and blood, so get your blood

pumping. Your movement will break you out of a lull or

routine, increasing your heart rate and releasing adrenaline,

which fuel your thinking.

True story: Once while brainstorming ideas for the car maker Mini, we were absolutely stuck. A room full of creatives, no ideas, and a deadline coming fast. We'd been sitting there all day, and that was only making our ideas worse. Luckily, someone randomly tossed a football into the room — something you wouldn't find odd in the creative department of an ad agency, I guess. As soon as the football hit a designer's fingertips, he had an idea. He tossed it to the next person, and they built on the idea. Soon, the ball was flying around the room, and the ideas were back. We spent hours in the room, and the winning idea came in minutes, only after we started moving our bodies.

So, grab a football, or grab your extremely warm, low-cost, environmentally-friendly Patagonia Human Jacket, and get your butt moving. Escape the usual distractions in front of you, and ignite some blood and adrenaline in your body. Besides, if you're at your desk, you're probably going to screw around online. Trap yourself in your own mind by getting away from tech, but still feel free to explore the world around you. There, you'll find new sounds, new places, new faces, and a bit of fresh air that will liven up your thinking. Just remember to record your ideas or they may get lost out there.

Dumb Brainstorming Tip #17: Make mashups.

Find fresh ideas in old places by thinking like a DJ, but like...less lame. Take people, places, things, objects, and platforms, then remix them in new and novel ways. "It's like UberEats...but for books and magazines!" "It's a tattoo parlor....for kids!" "It's an Amazon Echo....attached to a drone!" Do the same with stories. "It's Terminator meets Mary Poppins!" By combining story elements and commonly known concepts, we instantly feel more connected to the idea, no matter how bad it is, and our mind explodes with more ideas as it fills in the blanks, like "Does it mean the nanny is a Terminator? Wasn't that the premise for Terminator 2: Judgement Day?" Yes, yes it was.

Dumb Brainstorming Tip #18: Act it out.

Put yourself in the shoes of your characters or readers by actually acting out a scene or a day in their life. Talk like them, move like them, think like them. You'll loosen up, find some empathy and understanding, and maybe even discover something new about them and what you're working on. Be the character, be the consumer. For example, brilliant, award-winning Writer of TV, film, and stage, Aaron Sorkin, is known for crafting dialogue and drama by doing this very thing. In fact, he once famously broke his own nose while acting out a scene in his bathroom. So, lock yourself in your bathroom, and talk to yourself in the mirror, but try not to break your own nose, or anything else. It's not weird! Aaron Sorkin does it. You think you're better than Aaron Sorkin?!?! That guy broke his own nose for your entertainment. How is that weird?

If acting as a character or consumer is outside your comfort zone, try just immersing yourself in their world in other ways, like reading their content, listening to their music, or even putting on something they would wear. It's all about getting outside yourself to try to relate to them a little better. Consider the old adage of walking a mile in someone's shoes, and actually walk a mile in their shoes. For example, while working at MTV,

I was writing for a show targeted at teenage girls. The problem

was...I am not, nor was I ever, a teenage girl. So, I had to work

to understand them better. I had to find their perspective, use

their language, and then write in a way that they could relate to.

So, I consumed their content, and one day riding home on the

subway, while reading the latest issue of Teen magazine, with its

bright pink cover and the latest cute boy's photo, I realized this

is a very weird thing for me, a white guy in his late 20s, to be

reading in public. Then, I remembered I was on the NYC

subway and was therefore obviously the most normal person

around.

Dumb Brainstorming Tip #19: Sleep on it.

Do your research, do some b-storming, and then get away from

the challenge for a full night. While you're sleeping and are

distracted, your subconscious mind will work to solve the

problem for you. Let it do its work and let whatever dreams

come your way inspire you, but keep a pen and paper nearby, or

else you might lose what you thought of through the night.

Dumb Brainstorming Tip #20: Time yourself.

Without a deadline, you're more likely to get distracted or

attempt to craft the perfect idea in your head instead of actually

putting many good ideas down on the page to develop. Don't

waste your time looking for more inspiration or trying to build

on something when you should be coming up with more.

Instead, work in short bursts of time where you aim to deliver a

specific number of ideas. Change up your time periods and

number of ideas. Aim small at first to get warmed up, and then

amp up your target, like 100 ideas in a minute.

Is 20 enough? Sure, you got it. Let's move on...

Writing With Heart

"I've had a sign over my typewriter for over 25 years now,

which reads 'Don't think!'

You must never think at the typewriter — you must feel.

Your intellect is always buried in that feeling anyway.

Don't think. Thinking is the enemy of creativity.

It's self-conscious, and anything self-conscious is lousy."

- Ray Bradbury

Many Writers suffer from, or complain about, writer's block. It stops us from finishing big projects, and stifles the small ones, as well. But, big reveal here, there is no such thing as writer's block. There's only laziness, fear, and overthinking stuff. You're just using the wrong part of your mind at that moment.

Writing with Heart is the simple solution. As the wild, wondering, and wandering part of yourself, writing with the Heart is less about planning and outlining, and more about opening a fire hydrant of words and ideas, regardless if they're useful or "correct." A so-called "block" is a stoppage of words, so to overcome it, you must deliver words — it's that simple. You have to deliver those words in whatever way you can, but the easiest is merely to stop thinking about them, and just feeling them, allowing your random feelings, ideas, and subconscious thought flow onto the page. You don't have to use any of it, but at least the block is gone.

Your charge through this stage of writing is just to think less and feel more. Do not worry, do not edit, do not plan ahead. Never use writer's block as an excuse. The only way to do it is to do it. When you're stuck, the only way through it is through it. Just keep going. Put words on the page, worry about them later. Stop overthinking it and write. And, the following tips and techniques will help you do just that. They will help you escape your own mind, freeing yourself from methodical Head, and allowing you to bypass the block. You will learn to unleash ideas faster, without critique. Then, in later sections, you'll learn how to consolidate those ideas, give them structure and form, and focus your thinking and energy to drive you toward a more complete piece of writing.

The Braindump

The great conqueror of so-called writer's block, the Braindump is the most valuable tool a Writer can have, and yet it's also most certainly the one that's first abandoned. Simply, your Dump will be a stream of thoughts onto the page that will become your notes, regardless of what you're writing. It's where you input these ideas and information so as to not have to process and incubate them in your own head, because the reality of writer's block is that If there's no output, there was never enough input.

Proper incubation of writing never happens in the mind, and it rarely occurs in a linear fashion. It happens on the page. If you wait for the beautiful sentence, it will never come. If you try to craft it in your brain, by the time you get to the period, you'll have lost the beginning. Even if you attempt to craft a single short, simple email in your brain, by the time you get to the signature, the first sentence is long gone. It's like trying to remember a phone number. Seven numbers, okay, but toss an area code on there and we're done. How foolish of us to think we can write something without writing it down when we can't even remember full phone numbers. That's because your brain can only hold, process, and remember so much at a given time. As much as you believe you can create and craft an idea and it's written form in your brain, you're wrong. So, the more you Dump, the more opportunity you create for yourself and your work. The effort is to not ever try to write in your own brain. You have to take the dumber approach and just write it down.

Let's try it. Craft an email in your brain, right now, this very moment. Make it to a close friend. Make it pithy and relatable, but also make sure it solves a problem or has a clear call to action. I'll wait...

....You better be doing it...

....I know you're not...

....Ugh, fine, you suck....

Ok, if you played along then as you considered your

words and you built your message, you likely crafted something

amazing, yet as you continued on, that prior sentence, that killer

line you created before you moved onto the next, it certainly

faded. You might not have realized it at first. You thought you

were crushing it. But, when you went back to fix that great line

back there, you struggled to put it back together, and just doing

that made the rest of it vanish, as well. What a mess. You should

have just listened to me.

Your brain cannot comprehend and process that much

information while also making it exceptional, but for some

strange reason, we all still try to write in our minds, not on the

page. For some reason we think we're better than that. We think

we're so advanced in our ability to write a simple old email that

we can do it in the same brain that only remembers one phone

number these days. That's why putting it all on "paper" allows you to effectively store everything. Once you accept your

cognitive limitations and work from the Dump, you're free to

write more freely and wildly on the page, not in your brain.

Better out than in, as they say.

The Dump Doc

This gem of a writing tool exists as a Google Doc or similar

digital word processing document that allows you to write as

much as you can on a topic so as to put it on the page and not

try to leave it in your head. Other Dump locations include

Word, iPhone Notes, email drafts, and a classic piece of paper.

If you struggle with "writing" in any way, the Braindump

is where you tell yourself that it isn't writing at all; it's just jotting

some stuff down in a Google Doc. You can call it stream of

consciousness if you'd like. I call it "taking a dump" because I'm

a classy fella. But also, because calling it that is not at all

glamorous of a phrase, it's therefore more approachable, and

more achievable. A Dump lets you avoid the vast blank page

and that evil blinking cursor — it throws you forward into the work. With the Dump, there are no worries, no complications, no pretence, no straight lines you're forced to follow. You're just taking a good ol' dump. Everyone does it! It's your time, your space, your business. No one is watching, no one needs to know what happens, so there is no need to worry. It's even less pressure than taking a real dump in the workplace because it's much quieter and your pants are on, maybe.

Ok, back to business: writing is a creative act, and all too often we see creativity as something formulaic, something that requires outlines, process, and thought. But from all my years as a Writer, creative director, and TV producer, I've found that taking a Dump is the closest thing I've ever seen to a creative process. That's because, in its nature, it's meant to be raw creativity flowing freely onto the page where it can be stored, processed, and edited. Look into that chaos and you will in fact start to see patterns within. That means, the only process is to allow yourself to be free, to embrace the chaos with an open mind. Once you're taking your Dump, you'll be shocked by how quickly you can unload all kinds of shit, and somehow end up writing whatever you intended in the process. The act of freely writing allows you to solve problems through trial & error and an overall "shotgun approach." It's not a targeted shot, not a linear path, but a wide and wild shot that will hit enough of the target to get the job done. It moves up and down, backwards and forwards, and every which way, and that frenetic movement is what actually drives it forward. And, regardless of its complexity and disorder, you can always come back in later with some thoughtful editing to finish off the rest of the target that you're firing at — you don't have to hit it dead one immediately. With a Dump, you have unlimited ammunition. (Got my NRA readers locked in now! 'Bout time they started using their words.)

Throughout the length of your writing project, this Dump Doc will be a source for ideas, words, and phrases. It will be full of inspiration and content for you to pull from. You'll always be able to return to it, especially when you look to revise based on feedback. So, with the existence of this Dump, you can immediately recall those thoughts you had hours, days, weeks, months ago. The challenge then becomes, what in the hell do you do in the meantime with all this crap you just dumped out? That's where structure comes in — the forming and reforming of creative information, because good writing is just good editing. But, we'll cover that later in this book.

Dumb Writing Tip #4: Don't get it right, get it written.

Writers struggle most to put words on the page when they obsess over crafting the most finely tuned linguistic masterpiece ever to have been written. Don't do that. There's too much to remember and filter. Draft & craft. Fill the page, fix it later. It all starts with the words on the screen. It all starts with you taking a big Dump.

How to take a Dump:

1. Open a new Google Doc or similar clean sheet for storing information and ideas.

2. Start writing. Write everything and anything. This is your space to unleash it all.

How much do I write in my Braindump?

Good question. My general rule of thumb is that I give myself as much as half of my overall writing time to Dump and write freely onto the page throughout that time, which means if I estimate that I have two days to write, I'll Dump for one, while never questioning it or feeling like I'm procrastinating. You really have to feel comfortable having nothing that looks anywhere near finished for long stretches of time. If a novel roughly takes a year, give yourself a as many as six months to focus on nothing but ideas and free-flowing Dumps. If you Dumped correctly, when you actually get into crafting that novel, you will find it already exists in raw form inside your Dump — the work is there, it just doesn't look like it, yet. The next six months will just be cleaning up and structuring all of the ideas, plot points, dialogue, character descriptions, or whatever else you already had in there just waiting to be made sense of.

By Dumping well, whatever I'm supposed to be writing will be in there, in some form. It just won't be in any sort of order — only you will be able to feel it in there waiting for you, like a Renaissance sculptor seeing the statue in a piece of marble. If you have to write more, it means you didn't Dump

enough. Don't short-change yourself by limiting the time you

spend in the Dump stage. This is Disney's first room, and all

other rooms depend upon it, so give it time to work. Quality

comes from quantity.

People are too often scared that this collection of

random thoughts will be discovered and read aloud, like a diary.

But, the wonderful thing about Google docs is that you don't

have to share, and when you're done writing, you can delete it or

pretend it never existed. I have countless Google Docs stored up

that I've never revisited, but when they were in use, they were

absolutely priceless to my work. Likewise, your Dumps will not

be studied, reviewed, or critiqued. There will be no autopsy or

audit. They are yours and yours alone. So write freely, and treat

them as the priceless canvases they are for you, the Writer.

Additionally, Braindumps are not limited to big writing

exercises, like novels or scripts. You can use a Dump sheet even

for emails. Though, sometimes I overthink this and feel that

Google Docs are a real investment in what I'm writing, like I'm fully committing to it once that document exists. Therefore, I use a Gmail draft. It's smaller, feels like just an email, and therefore eliminates some of the pressure. The Notes app on your phone, email drafts, your notebook — anything can be a Dump sheet for you, so use whatever helps you complete your work.

Dumb Writing Tip #5: Steal, but don't like...*steal.*

Let everything inspire your writing, and that means copy & pasting quotes, lyrics, poems — whatever feels like it will guide your words. Put them all in your Dump. Fill it up with other people's ideas. Every idea is a good idea in your Dump. Fill as many pages as you can. Just be sure to use different fonts and colors in order to separate the work that you paste in so as to prevent plagiarism. If someone else has already said it, but it's guiding your thinking and making your work better, just color it red to remind yourself that it's not in fact your thought. Also, use the comments to make notes to yourself, like "This is a good intro!" Or, "This needs more research." Never delete from your

Dump. It was valuable enough to put it in there, so it may be valuable again later. But, as you no longer need your added comments, you can resolve them to declutter. Otherwise, comments make a great guide as your Dump may start to get heavy. (Imagine the weird search value this book is going to have when it goes digital. It's going to be very popular in the "Writers with IBS" community. Hi, everyone! How are your butts? Good.)

Dumb Writing Tip #6: Use shorthand.

Remember, this is your Braindump, your notes, and no one else's. That means only you have to understand it. So, to get ideas out faster, play with creating a shorthand language for yourself. This way, you can write faster without having to overthink or over-edit yourself. For example, whenever I'm writing a brand name or referring to a person in my Dump, I use numbers. The main subject is always 1. Secondary subjects are obviously 2. So, while working on content for the Stearns & Foster mattress company, it would have been super annoying, and taken way too much time, to write that long name out every time. But, by just writing "1" in my notes anytime I wanted to use the name, I could quickly move on to the actual idea. Plus, if I were to ever worry about someone reading my Dump, they would never understand it anyways. They're all in some weird language that only I can read. It's job security that way, as the working documents for all projects are coded, only unlockable by the key in my brain. (Insert sinister laugh...here.)

Another shorthand technique is not using vowels, which is actually kinda fun because your laptop or mobile device will try to guess what you're writing, so when you revisit it, you're going to get a laugh from the absurdity of your notes. Jst wrtng wrds with n vwls stll mks sns 2 th brn smhw. Mst b fckn mgc. However, you might find yourself thinking too hard about not adding vowels, so instead just focus on writing as quickly as possible without any grammar or spelling holding you back.

You can also use what I call "Christopher Walken-ing," which is writing without any punctuation — just letting the thoughts flow without worrying about them being written correctly. This name comes from the legend that the unique cadence in his acting is due to him not reading the punctuation as it's written in scripts, causing odd inflections points in the read.

Whatever techniques you use to write simpler faster, the act of shortening will most certainly cause confusing mistakes in your writing. However, you'll find that by writing it by hand (writing by hand or typing), you'll somehow remember. The act of putting it down, whether on paper or screen, will create a mental marker to help call back your idea when you read back through your notes. The trick is to try different things and make it your own. Whatever you need to write better and faster is correct, regardless if it's confusing or inconvenient to someone else. This is your document and your space to explore your ideas. Screw everyone else.

Dumb Writing Tip #7: Write what you know.

This is not the famous adage of writing only what you know. This is the literal form of writing down what you know in your brain, so beyond just a flow of creative crap plopping onto the page, put everything you *know* down in this sheet, EVERYTHING. Leave nothing out. Write down what you're doing. Write the one single thing you're trying to say and do. Write every piece of information you know in regards to this bit of writing. Just by putting it down on the paper, your brain is free to focus on what's next, not what is or was. So, if this is for a client, write about the client. What do you know? What do you think? How do you feel? How do you think they feel? Is this a new experience for you, for them, for the reader? Everything is valuable. And, putting it on the page certainly doesn't mean you're committed to it. It's just some pixels that no one will read, and that can be deleted with absolute ease.

Dumb Writing Tip #8: Explain it like you're a total idiot.

We're obviously overthinking everything in our work and lives, so by simplifying things for ourselves, even for a moment, we can finally see things more clearly. So, pretend like you know nothing. You're an absolute moron who needs everything laid out simply. Overthink nothing, explain everything. Hit on every detail as if you're explaining it to someone else, someone who's not as smart as you, some fool.

What are you doing? Why are you doing it? Where is it going? Every answer, every thought, goes on the page. Whatever you're trying to write, write it out to yourself, in great detail, like you have no goddamn clue what you're talking about. Don't worry about grammar, punctuation, or spelling, for now. Mistakes are not only ok, they're great. Make countless mistakes. Make glorious mistakes! No one is paying attention to your Dump, so explain it as in-depth as possible, clearly laying it all out from an empowered position — someone who knows versus someone who doesn't — without any fear, since no one but you will read it. You'll probably write a good portion of your goal in the process. That's because we easily forget how much readers prefer simplicity and authenticity over fancy prose.

If you're writing for a client, write about them. Who are they? What are they like? What are their challenges? Pretend you know absolutely nothing about this project and explain it, no matter how ridiculous it seems. Every detail matters, no matter how stupid. It's almost certain that none of this will end up in your finished product, but just the act of putting it on the page allows it to be considered. It prevents us from reaching out too far without remembering where we stand, what is true, what, and whom this is all for. This is to keep us grounded. This is a guide for the work and a foundation to work from, so start simply, and don't over-complicate things early. That only ensures things are complicated later.

Dumb Writing Tip #9: Write your one thing.

The Dump is the tip I most often recommend, but it's also absolutely the thing everyone seems to forget or overlook. That's because sometimes the act of Braindumping is considered too time consuming when a writing project is small, like an email. However, there's a faster option. It's like a mini speed Dump. It's to just write the one thing you're trying to say, in no more than a sentence. If you use 'and' or 'or' then it's not one thing anymore. It's two things. Simplify.

One of the times I saw this dumb technique used immediately and effectively was at an advertising agency where I was helping the account team unlock their inner Writers, particularly through their client relations, and specifically through cutting down the amount of time they spent crafting emails to clients. One single email was being estimated to take an hour. AN HOUR! Ridiculous! A whole hour just for one email?!? What a waste of time — especially when they can call the client much faster! That's not at all valuable to the employee who is writing and rewriting an email when they could be thinking about growing the client's business or elevating their own capabilities as an employee and teammate. The challenge for these account representatives when it came to the Braindump was that it was time consuming, especially since the purpose was to do more with their time, not simply to do something else with it. So, I offered this Speed Dump option based on finding their One Thing.

To get their thoughts out faster, but without converting an hour writing an email to an hour Braindumping an email, I asked them to just write down what the email intended to do — just that one line, that one sentence that expressed the reason they were writing anything at all, nothing else. They could try writing it many times in the same email draft, but each version was to be a simple expression of their intention in one sentence, no more. I prefaced that this is meaningless. It's just to put something down on the page to work with, much like the more comprehensive Braindump. Just write it down, and we can delete it later. The first step is to actually write it, though, not have it in your head. In there, it's worthless.

Once they wrote it, with that simple line on the page, I then asked them to add some flare to it, some humanity, like an inside joke, an emoji, or a reference to their last conversation. Boom, two things on the page with little thought, and that was it.

When they reread what they put down, they realized that that was it. A little Head with a little Heart for flourish and it was the email they wanted to write all along, but it only took a minute, not an hour. Why? Because they always were overthinking it. They were worried about so many things that even if they thought of a good email, it soon became clouded by fear and anxiety — "How will they respond? Am I coming across as too robotic? Not robotic enough? Am I being too personable? What will my boss think if they see this? Oh, crap, I forgot what I was going to write."

By finding their One Thing, they were no longer overthinking it, or drafting it in their mind where they consistently lose it. They put it simply on the page and they were done. The day before, they averaged one email an hour. The day after, they would be able to average sixty emails and hour, if they wanted to or needed to write that many. By opening up that time, they could focus more on building the account, finding new accounts, or exploring their own creativity more.

Start with the one thing you're doing with your writing.

What's the one thing you absolutely want to get across, say, or ask? What story are you trying to tell? What message do you want the reader to receive? Don't overthink it. Ask yourself what success looks like in this email. If it's to get a response, maybe feedback on some work, then your One Thing is directly asking for that feedback and/or offering the results of not getting that feedback. Don't overthink it. Start with what you need, what success is, or what failure is, and just put it on the page. Work from there. Consolidate it down into one thesis, or comment, or demand, or question, or kickass line, but always get it down to one single simple sentence, or you're still overthinking it.

Dumb Writing Tip #10: Write your one word.

If you're in a hurry, the One Thing Speed Dump is a solution, but when you're exploring the full Braindump for all its glory, you still want to find your One Word. It's the heart, and soul, and magic running through your work, because this Dump is a place for your Heart to play, so your One Word will help represent all the things that you feel about this thing you're writing. One single word, and when you look at it, you just get what you're doing and why. It should be that powerful, to you at least.

To find your One Word, collect the words already out in the world that inspire you and that makes this work special — quote, lyrics from your favorite songs, lines from great movies. Collect them all in your Dump.

Visit the greats, like Tennyson, Shakespeare, Sorkin, Whitman, and Thompson — anyone who moves you. Anyone who was a master of the craft of language expression, those with very different styles, will be the ones worth exploring. Reading authors from different cultures, times, and mediums will expose you to different rhythms and patterns, and it will make your word timeless, not trendy.

Give yourself time to explore these works. Capture everything that moves you in any way, every word, and absorb them. You, as a Writer, will benefit, I promise. Put your favorites in an all-time Dumpsheet. It's the all-star of Braindumps that you can use on any project. Fill it with quotes

from your favorite Writers, or your favorite pieces by them. Let
it be your guide every damn day.

With all of these collected words, find the one thing that
reminds you of this thing you're writing. It doesn't have to be
exactly One Word. It can be a few — a short phrase or line that
lights you up inside. Just know as you search your Dump sheet:
It's in there somewhere, if you're opening up your soul even a
little bit. And, if you're open to it, it will just jump out at you. It
wants to be found. It's the thing that sounds similar to what
you're feeling, except you could never quite put your finger on it
before. It's the thing that just feels right now that you've found it.
Use the Heart, not the Head here. It doesn't need to be logical.
You gotta have fun with it, put your heart and soul into it, or the
reader never will. The one thing that speaks to the soul of the
work is always my first step. Most of the time, whether it's within
a poem, a quote, or musical lyrics, when I find that one single
word that captures what I'm trying to day, I get excited and want
to share. But, no one ever feels it the same way I do, which is

fine. That's why I'm writing this and not them. This is my one single thing. It's meant to move me, not them.

Too weird? Too bad. Let's look at an example: Working with brands requires the use of these heartfelt words and lines. In a world where humanity, authenticity, and approachability are demanded of brands, my work in advertising, as well as brand development and strategy, is fueled by these core, foundational creative elements that inspire greater things. When building a brand, the first thing I always do to find this hearty, powerful, intentional work is to break the brand down into just one word — one single word that expresses what this brand is, and who it's people are, and why they all exist in the world. That One Word becomes my beacon, my North Star guiding my whole Dump and subsequent works.

Then, with that One Word, I read quotes containing that word. Brainyquote.com and Goodreads.com are much-used bookmarks for exploring quotes, and as I find them, I copy and paste them into my Dump. I make them big and bold, because I want them to imprint in my mind every time I scroll past. Pro

Tip: don't just choose great quotes, choose personalities that can back-up the quote in case it so heavily inspires the work that people can see it, or if the client asks where the thought came from. Because, if you end up moved by some Austrian guy named Hitler, it doesn't matter if you leave his name off. The essence of his quote has the chance to peek through, and yes, I have had other writers recognize what inspired me. Though not a single phrase was used, a fellow writer once read an ad of mine and said, "You read Roosevelt's *Man in the Arena* right before writing this, didn't you?" I had, and there are minds like that out there, so don't get caught being inspired by Hitler. You can use that piece of advice for things other than writing, if you'd like.

In terms of boiling brands down to a word, you might choose Win for Nike. For Casper mattresses, it's Simpler. For Harley Davidson, it might be Gang, or Tribe, or Freedom. For a gourmet gift basket brand I was helping to develop, I chose Napa, not because it made sense to anyone else, but because I was using Napa Valley wineries for my beacon. Napa Valley's tasting experiences, their labels, their language, their mood, their colors, their music — these were all things tied to this premier and tangible industry that helped me guide this emerging brand into existence. And, it was for me and me alone. It was meaningless to anyone else. But, for me, it was my Heart side looking for how things felt, whether or not it was logical. With that word, I Googled, and browsed, and read the lyrics and quotes. I watched videos of vintners, which is a weird word. I read what they talked about reading to get into their hearts and minds. Along the way, I came to the quote that further inspired me from inside my Dump:

"To live content with small means. To seek elegance rather than luxury, and refinement rather than fashion. To be worthy not respectable, and wealthy not rich. To study hard, think quietly, talk gently, act frankly, to listen to stars, birds, babes, and sages with open heart, to bear all cheerfully, do all bravely, await occasions, hurry never. In a word, to let the spiritual, unbidden and unconscious, grow up through the common. This is to be my symphony."

-- William Ellery Channing

Seemingly dumb because it wouldn't make sense for others, and therefore was never offered to the client, or the team, it was always there for me. It was mine. It was a part of my Dump, inspiring me whenever I saw it. With it, I could feel the brand, and just by seeing it, I was once again reignited with inspiration and possibility, connection, and understanding. They spoke gently and never hurried, but instead were graceful and poised, while still being connected to the Earth and healthy, organic foods. They were elegant, not luxurious, and therefore stood out from all the competitors who had to remind people that they were luxurious.

My mind didn't need to remember this quote, or even remind me of it. It was always accessible to me, guiding me when I needed to revisit it. Later, anything the brand would do or say, I could feel Napa in it. I could see Napa. It wasn't always wine in the baskets, but for me, opening a basket would always be a Symphony. It would feel elegant and refined, as guided by the quote powered by Napa — my One Word. From there, the work would be all Heart.

Not feeling it? No worries. You can straight-up steal the word from someone else. When working with clients, account people, or other creatives, do not hesitate from stealing words and ideas from them. Their thoughts and opinions are more palatable to your creative mind when they come forward as ideas and not critiques. So, ask questions early. Capture what they say and steal it because they probably don't even know they're saying it. The One Word might be in their Head or Heart already, you just have to dig for it. That way, you are instantly aligned. They agree with you on the One Word, and they don't even know you're stealing it, let alone that it exists.

As an example, many years ago I was helping a startup define their brand for the world. Its founder was a hands-on, opinionated entrepreneur, so I knew that whatever I offered he would tear it apart, because he didn't build it himself. My challenge was to articulate his baby to the world for years if not decades, so it had to be perfect, not just as a representation of the brand but as a reflection of him and everything he's built or will build in the future. So, long before I wrote a word, I went for a walk with him. I let him talk about the heart of the business and brand he created. In this conversation, he spoke from the Heart, revealing the underlying truth and beauty of it all, which he could never express otherwise because he was always selling it, not speaking emotionally about it. Particularly he said one word over and over. They always do. (In fact, every time he said it, he would turn to look at me as if he was putting emphasis on it) It was the One Word, the one thing he was trying to do beyond make money. If you find that word, or phrase, and steal it, then use it throughout your work, they'll see it. They'll see themselves in it, whether they realize it or not. They'll feel it, and somehow know it's right, because they see their vision in it. In the case of the startup, I used his language and One Word throughout, but built on it. I made it more dynamic and functional as a consumer brand. But, at its heart was his expression. He was the one who gave it to me, he made my job much easier, he just didn't realize it.

So, if you use the One Thing and break your work down to one single sentence, which is hard enough, you can then break it down to one single word. What is the One Word that speaks to the soul of your work? For a brand, what do you feel when you consider or interact with them? If you wanted the reader to walk away with one word, what would it be? If you can't nail down one word, guess what? Yep, you're overthinking everything. This is your time to try different things, so pick the first word that stands out to you and explore it. Find music that sings about the things you're feeling. Find your favorite writers writing about it already. Collect everything, even if they aren't clearly connected, and put it all in your Dump. You don't have to use it, but once it's in there, it's there for you in case you want it. There's no harm in putting it in there, but if you don't, it will eventually cease to exist inside your mind, and therefore offers no value to you or your writing. One Word. It's not all that hard.

Dumb Writing Tip #11: Call it what it is.

Whatever you're using to Braindump, actually title it Dump, not a draft, a Dump. Write it at the top, literally. Yeah, it's simple, it's maybe stupid, but it works. This allows you to drop thoughts and ideas and words here without worrying about it being something it's not. It gives you the freedom to explore, not to write. This is not the first draft. I repeat: This is not the first draft. This is a Braindump. The draft comes later, so don't make it be something it's not, or you will only trip yourself up. You'll look at this massive pile of random words and thoughts and you will think you're nowhere, when in fact you are right where you need to be in the long process that is writing.

Dumb Writing Tip #12: Believe.

At this stage in your journey, things could look bleak. I mean, really, if you look at it, you have nothing but a whole lot of notes. It would be easy to give up now. After all, there's such a long way to go still. There's so much work to be done. It can be overwhelming. That's why you just have to tell yourself that you'll get it done. Believe in yourself and your abilities or no one else will. Remind yourself you'll get there, say it out loud and believe in it, because the whole path getting there is going to be complicated and confusing and scary. Writing is not easy, ever. But, you will get it done. Solutions will come. Language will flow. You just have to believe.

Write Crazy

"Writer's block results from too much head. Cut off your head.

Pegasus, poetry, was born of Medusa when her head was cut off.

You have to be reckless when writing.

Be as crazy as your conscience allows."

-- Joseph Campbell

With your One Thing, your One Word, and your collection of others' great writing to inspire you and reflect the soul of what you're writing, you have to write madly, openly, and freely — in an unabashed frenzy, free from strain or structure. You've started the engine, so now it's time to hit the open roads and drive the hell out of that damn car. Don't think, just write. Write your thoughts and feelings, not a blog post, or a script, or an email. There is no structure yet. This is your time to infuse creativity, and emotion, and passion, and energy, and pure shit, because shit is good at this stage. Shit should be celebrated! You can fix bad pages, but you can't fix no pages, so shit away! Put something on the page, anything, and you can work with it later.

If you need one good line, write a few bad ones and consider what makes them bad. The truth is that by writing in multiples, you're likely to accidentally write one you like. This is why, in advertising, creative directors demand 50-100 headlines and taglines from their copywriters. It's not to be mean. Well, sometimes it's to be mean. But, mostly, it's to get their ideas out onto the page so they aren't trying to write in their own heads. If they write 100 headlines for a print ad and actually write them down while doing it, only about five will be any good. If they try to write five in their head, it'll probably take the same amount of time, and maybe one single good one, maybe, will even be remembered. The difference is in being able to see what's on the page — what's good and what's bad? What's working and what isn't? What can you build on or deconstruct? These questions can only be asked when you're working with more ideas, not less. The Head needs something to work off of, and that means the Heart must deliver some magic. So, write away. Write freely, with no bounds.

Even try just writing single words. Literally, just single words stacked on top of one another. Use word association and write every word you can think of related to your topic. Spend time in a thesaurus and write out synonyms for the words you come up with. See what journeys that takes you on. The more words you write, the more you have to work with, so why limit yourself right from the start?

Use the dumb tips before and after this, fill the page with everything you got, and don't watch the clock. Remember that to get to a handful of good ideas, you're going to have to write a hundred, and that's okay. In this Dump, bad ideas are good. Bad writing is great, because now is not the time to worry, stress, think, or edit. You're free to suck terribly, no one is watching.

Still feeling stuck? Ask yourself questions, have an idiotic conversation with yourself for fun, and create similes and metaphors to allow yourself to see things from different sides, adding depth and different perspectives to your point of view, while also adding some creative flavor.

Example:

- **What do I want to express with this book?** *I want people to not overthink their writing so they write more, better, and faster.*

- **How does it make you feel?** *Worried that I'm actually under-thinking it all, and everything I do that I think is clever is all just crap advice, or not as insightful as I imagined, and is therefore going to be torn apart by this person right here reading it. (Yeah you.)*

- **Make connections based on that. What is that like?** *This book might be like toilet paper still on the roll. I think it's useful, but people are still probably going to shit on it.*

- **Now I'm worried you're using too many poop puns. I thought you were a professional?** *How dare you! That's just a shitty thing to say, and what do you know anyway!?!?*

- **I'm you, dummy.** *Yeah, well, you're a real asshole.*

Much like explaining it to yourself like you're an idiot, having a conversation with yourself adds a fresh perspective, albeit a weird one, which allows you to see your work differently. It's similar to how someone new to a project can immediately see the mistake or a way to make something better as soon as they walk in the room. It's incredibly annoying but it always happens and it's always helpful , no matter what you're working on (even if you don't like to admit it). Those people have a magical power to see what you can't see because they're not trapped deep in the weeds like you are. They're swooping in with fresh, unbiased eyes — something you're preventing yourself from doing despite the amazing ability for your creative mind to shift perspectives in a moment. So, remember to find new ways to shift points of view. Review your own work by asking questions, explaining it to yourself in dumb ways, and just get it onto the page where you are more likely to catch mistakes and improve your own writing before someone else can annoyingly swoop in to do it for you.

Dumb Writing Tip #13: Write crap for 20 minutes.

Block out 20 minutes for yourself to just write nothing. Accept that it's going to be totally useless and will never lead to the final product. It's not meant for that. It's meant to open the door for more ideas. 20 minutes, that's it. Sit down and write, anything. Just stop thinking, and by thinking, I mean the self-critique, the planning ahead, the anxiety, the fear, the need for perfection — everything brewing in your brain that prevents the words from flowing. No barriers, no restrictions, no judgement or questioning looks from anyone. Just 20 hot minutes of wide-open words. It's an incubation stage for ideas, but make sure it's all on the page. See where your mind takes you. If it stalls, try changing perspective. Talk to yourself. Listen to the words in your brain. Focus on them. Oftentimes, you'll get so caught up in the words that you'll keep going well past 20 minutes. That's because you're blocked when you're trying to write everything, but when you're trying to write nothing, you're free. So, write as if you'll never be read. Write freely, and damn the critics. Be mindless, let inspiration drive. See where it takes you. Be open to the journey and know that it will take time, and that that's perfectly fine. Allow the curious Feeler inside you to explore possibilities and ask unanswered questions. Then, have the mindful Thinker make attempts at answering those questions. Allow one to work and then the other. And don't write any of this in your own brain. Put it on the page. Just let ideas exist on the page. Write it and see what happens. When your words are out in the world, they can open doors. They're goddamn magic.

Dumb Writing Tip #14: Write with pictures.

Having trouble bringing ideas to life inside your own head with just words? Those weird one-on-one conversations just not happening? That's ok. You may be a visual person. You need pictures, images, colors, and shapes to help form your thoughts. Your Dump needs to be more visually appealing. Without this, words get jumbled in your mind unless they're funnelled through drawing, sketching, doodling, etc. In meetings, people might think you're not paying attention, when in reality, this *is* you paying attention! You listen with your hands and eyes, not your ears. So, break out your notebook and Dump through pictures. Get fancy with an iPad Pro, or go retro with some MS Paint. Color with crayons with your actual hands, on actual paper, and don't stop there — frame them! Let them be artifacts of your work — tangible creations to reflect your soon-to-be digital words and ideas.

Dumb Writing Tip #15: Write with your mouth.

Writing freely without an inner editor telling you to slow down, or to stop being weird, is extremely difficult. So if the Braindump isn't coming easily, don't write, just talk. Get away from that insistent bastard, the blinking cursor, and any environment that reminds you that you're supposed to be working. Free your mind by freeing yourself. Then, pull out your phone and use a recording app to record your rant. Go for a walk and talk as if you're talking to a friend on the phone.

Explain what you want to write, what you want to say, what you want it to do. Get it out of your brain. Then, use a digital transcription service to transcribe it for you. Now all of your words, ideas, and intentions are right there on the page and you have something to work with. However, and this is important, do not try to start over. It's all there, everything you need. That is your Dump. It will be your foundation for your writing. Craft it into something, anything. You obviously had something to say, enough that you walked around talking to yourself like a crazy person! It's all right there, so don't let it die.

Dumb Writing Tip #16: Let your lil' idiot write.

If this were in the Head section later in the book, we'd be talking about this as deep focus, or being in a mental flow state. But, we're in the Heart section, so it's far more wacky and weird. That's because I firmly believe that there is another *you* in your brain. It's this whole other person with different talents and opinions and tastes. They're a benevolent secret self that's trapped inside your body with no clear voice or control, unless you give them the opportunity to come out and play.

Mine's in there, I know it! And he's a great Writer. I'm actually not a good Writer, at all, never have been. I didn't do well in college. I was told by my advisor not to even try. Yet, somehow I've made a living off of it. I even sold at least one copy of a book, which you're reading right now. That's because he gets it, man — my little guy, he gets it. He doesn't worry about what people think. He doesn't overthink *anything*. He just unleashes words onto the page. It's actually cool to witness. I'm just sitting there, not thinking at all, kinda zoning out, but words are appearing on the page. Sometimes they're good, most of the time they aren't, but there they are, right there, flowing, coming to life. I can't control it, or him, but I like it.

His name is Kevin, my little idiot who lives in my brain and writes for me. He's too dumb to understand critique or social pressures. He doesn't care what I want or what I think. He doesn't understand job security. He doesn't worry about us paying our bills. He just knows words, and that's it. He LOVES words. He never helps me anywhere else in life. He's just this dummy in my head who actively grabs onto words, ideas, and anything creative and he stores them up there for me. In everything I do, I'm the critic, I'm the judge, I'm the skunk, I'm the party-pooper, and Kevin...man, Kevin is the creative madman — an open hydrant of ideas. Gotta love Kev.

Oftentimes when someone comments on my writing, or asks questions, I can't respond because I don't really know what happened or why I made the decisions that I made. People think I'm being humble, but since when am I ever humble?!? I can't answer because I didn't actually write it. Kevin wrote it, not me. Someone will ask why I wrote something the way I did, or used that word specifically. I have no friggin idea, man! I didn't actually write it, my mind's a blank right now! Someone will compliment a piece of writing, and I feel like I can't even take ownership or praise. Aren't you listening?! I didn't write it! For the Heads out there, I was in that hyper-focused flow state, which can slightly blur memory, but for you Hearts, I simply wasn't in charge. I didn't write those things. My boy Kevin did.

Plus, when things go wrong and I make mistakes or follow the wrong paths, I don't take credit or beat myself up over it, because it wasn't me. I didn't do it. It's not my fault. It was that idiot Kevin over there, wasting my precious time with his dumb words. My writing wasn't bad, HIS was! What an asshole. I'd totally fire him, if I could. But, he has tenure.

So, find that person in your brain. Get to know the little idiot in there. Trust your inner weirdo. Give them a name. Listen to them when they have something to share. Give up the wheel and let them drive for a bit. Feel the flow of ideas they can offer, and blame them if things go poorly.

Once you become acquainted with your inner idiot, like being in a deep meditative mental flow state, like musicians or a Navy SEAL sniper, writing with your idiot allows you to forget space and time in order to experience a form of intense hyper focus. Normally, you're in control, so you saying the words aren't right, or that you're wasting time, or wondering if it's 'they're' or 'their' is just slowing you down. You're getting in your own way. But, your little creative idiot up there in your head, they don't worry about these trivial things. They just want you to get out of their way. They want to write. It's why they exist. Let them do their thing.

Well said, Kev.

Dumb Writing Tip #17: Dress up for the words.

In order to disrupt fear and my own repeating routines, style, and existence, I've found myself making subtle changes during my writing days by "dressing up" for the work ahead. Now, be clear, this is not dressing up in the way it's commonly used. I am certainly not in a suit & tie. I am instead in whatever I can find, from a pink cowboy hat to rainbow suspenders, in order to change my perspective.

In college, I would sneak over to a female friend's house next door and grab what I could — some Juicy sweatpants, check! Some big ol' fashionista sunglasses, got'em! Whatever I could quickly and easily get my hands on, I used them as tools to help myself fall deeper and deeper into myself. I was pure focus, driven by a force that is purely "me" or maybe purely

"Kevin." There were no expectations, no barriers, no prejudices, no preconceived notions, no rules. I was creating a small experience for myself, not trying to look or be cool, and not trying to prove anything to anyone. I didn't care what people thought of me, I was just in the moment, a conduit for words and ideas. I was telling myself that this moment is different — that I should do and see things differently while in this uniform.

Imagine my roommates' confusion seeing me at my computer dressed like this. They had to not only wonder why I was wearing a Speedo, but where did it come from and why didn't it fit very well? They were too scared to ask. And, worse for them was that I would never have explained it even if they asked, because this was my time. I was working. I was in the zone. I was dressing for myself, my muse, my dearest Kev-Kev, and my words, and nothing or no one else. I had no time for their mundane worries like being a normal human functioning in polite society. I had to write, dammit!

Elizabeth Gilbert, writer of brilliantly written books *Eat, Pray, Love* and *Big Magic* goes beyond the absurd to actually dress up for her ideas. With a dress, some jewelry, and some make-up, she doesn't just show up to write, she shows up to entice her creative muse. It's about the seduction of this creative magic that's floating around us. Impress it and maybe it'll join you as you work. Don't and maybe it'll go off and find someone else to inspire — someone who appears to be more interested in a collaboration — someone worthy of their creative, artistic powers.

Keep in mind, it doesn't have to be clothes, or props, either. It's more about creating a new mindset for yourself — a fresh perspective to put you into the right room for wild, freewheeling creativity. Aaron Sorkin, winner of all the screenwriting awards, takes as many as eight showers a day when he's writing. He does this as a redo, to start the day over fresh, to feel new again when he hits walls or is unhappy with his work. Each shower is a new day, a chance to wash away the bad writing from time past, and instead, feel refreshed and capable of looking forward with a renewed perspective. And, even if he is still writing poorly, at least he is clean, which not all working Writers can truthfully claim.

So, don't just write the words, entice, seduce, and interact with them by playing dress up. Literally grab things from the world around you — someone else's shoes, a funny hat, a jacket made from human hair — and put them on while you write. Dressing up in odd, unexpected, non-traditional outfits while you write will help you get outside yourself, to break your routines and sense of self. It's a way to see your world with new eyes, and to condition yourself to mentally switch mindsets — to forget the worries of the world for a bit. With a few random articles of clothing, you'll become someone else entirely, and maybe they have some fresh ideas.

Dumb Writing Tip #18: Less critiquing, more creating.

Don't you dare edit until it's ready. Write long and never critique when you should be filling the page. All good writing begins with terrible first efforts, but you need to start somewhere. When you're writing in this Dump, you're creating, and the prefrontal cortex of your brain is suppressed, which is linked to conscious self-monitoring. It's a simple switch. One turns on, and the other turns off. If one is working, the other is not. What that means is if you allow yourself to self-edit while being creative, the creative part of your brain is actually turning off. Actively trying to prevent yourself from making a mistake or come up with "dumb" ideas means no longer creating something new, so stop thinking so much. We make the mistake of thinking everything we write has to be a masterpiece. We forget that not only did the greats like Hemingway write crap now and then, but they believed in the art of the draft. They didn't turn a blank page into *The Sun Also Rises* by plopping down once and having it all figured out. They explored. They allowed themselves to make horrible mistakes. They crafted and shat all over the page, knowing they could come back later using their Head, and they could fix everything. But, they also knew that there was a time for creating and a time for critiquing, and they never worked together at the same time.

At some point, as a Writer, you yourself also have to become comfortable with writing badly and then exploring it, understanding it, learning from it. You can't hide from writing badly, no matter who you are. It's inevitable, it exists. You have to face it head-on. You have to see terrible sentences and ideas on the page and not be scared away. You have to ignore your ego — that one telling you that you're secretly the next great thing, the next great all-American novelist in disguise, just waiting to be discovered. You damn well may be, but you'll earn it by your final drafts, not your first, so be fearless. Be foolish in these dreams. Be flat-out dumb. Put bad, shameful, ridiculous things on the page. Work from there and remember that it's all deletable and private, and therefore a safe place to play with words and ideas.

Don't ever be precious about this. It's not your baby, yet. It's a creative free-for-all. You're attached to none of it. Laugh crazily while you burn through ideas. You're an insane person running naked, wild, and free — away from critics, rules, reviews, and opinions. Write with Heart, dammit. Have some fun because, here, in your draft, you're a puppy — curious and energetic, playing with everything, focusing on nothing, and occasionally peeing on the floor as you get overexcited. Don't expect great tricks from yourself here, just be. You're only a dumb little puppy and that's not a bad thing, it's a glorious thing. Everything is new, everything is wonderful. You will stumble over your giant paws and that is ok. This is a time for learning and exploration, and you're only at the beginning of your journey. You'll grow from here.

Dumb Writing Tip #19: Turn off your brain.

Writing with emotion and Heart is extremely difficult when so many of us are accustomed to thinking strategically and logically. Being truly free to transfer words to the page is not a simple switch we can flip, but we can try by finding routine ways of shutting down our mile-a-minute thoughts, if you have them.

For myself, 9gag.com is the trick. I browse straight-up dumb digital content for a few minutes, just scrolling past idiotic memes. Soon, I start to feel numb, like you feel after a solid gold Netflix binge, or by watching any primetime network TV multicam comedies for a minute. Through this 9gag scroll, I stop thinking about everything else going on in my life and work. I stop thinking about yesterday, or tomorrow, or lunch, or even whatever I was just worrying about, and I can transition into any piece of writing with a fresh, open, uninterrupted mind. Whatever I was doing before, whatever was on my mind, is gone now. I'm an empty vessel ready for words.

To go even further in calming your ADD brain with some structured procrastination, choose a series of sites that reflect what you'll be writing. If you're writing for moms, set aside some mom blogs. Writing for young millennials? Throw Buzzfeed up there. The point is to allow yourself the time to explore new worlds while also capturing language from your audience and forgetting the other stuff you were getting caught up in. Slowly, you begin to focus while also finding inspiration. And, with a simple, methodical scroll, and some websites that require little brain-power, you can lull yourself into a soothing, relaxing trance, allowing your Heart to take over for some writing fun.

Writing for an Existing Voice

Whether writing for brands as marketers, for individuals as content ghostwriters, or for fictional characters, it's not uncommon for Writers to be required to quickly adopt a variety of voices in our work. As you Dump, it helps to not only drop your thoughts and ideas onto the page, but also to *become* the voice you're speaking as in order to make sure it's accurate and truly reflecting that brand, person, or character.

Obviously, writing in different voices can be a great challenge, for anyone, no matter how experienced they are. When it comes to writing in different voices, let me say, I'm no expert, but I have done it quite a bit with everything from writing as a suburban mom to writing for Latino teenagers in a language I don't even speak. So these few steps are what have always worked for me.

1) Do The Research

Jumping right into the writing is a great way to simply craft for a voice or reader, but it's not a great way to write *as* them. Having an idea, interview, brief, and some notes is just the start. Go further.

I will watch videos, listen to recordings, read through emails, slack conversations, text messages, social feeds, and news articles. I look for every form of written or verbal communication I can find about the person I'm writing as, if it exists, and then I capture it in my Dump. For example, on a brand that was solely for moms, I read comments on news articles that got them fired up (I wanted to hear raw emotion and comments sections are great places to get unedited rants). I spent a lot of time on Pinterest. I pulled quotes from Nielsen studies about moms. I talked to my sister who is a mom. I watched the E! network. Throughout it all, I put everything I learned in one place until I had something that gave me a new perspective beyond myself. From my Dump, I was able to take the passion, language, and energy the moms brought forth and I wrote in a way that would not merely paint them with the "mom brush" but instead represented who they are beyond being just mom. But, it all began with thorough research and not mere assumptions. Never assume you know someone until you've done some work first.

For those writing as someone who does not have real-life embodiments to research and capture — a fictional character, for example — just attach real-life personas to the voice you're writing. If it's a cowboy, use real-life people who represent them, do research on them, and capture it. Maybe your cowboy has some Han Solo qualities, but with more humor. There's plenty of research available on Solo, so simply find your funny persona and combine traits for both in your Dump, where you can then sift through and determine what best represents this character you're speaking for.

2) Make a Profile

With all of your Dump-worthy content captured in one place, start studying it. You did the research, now look for patterns.

What words do they use often? Notice syllable usage, cadence,

inflection. Find common mistakes they make and wonder why.

Pay attention to punctuation. Do they speak fast, seemingly

without punctuation, or do they take long pauses? Listen for the

things that make them sound weird. Those are the things that

make them sound different from others and what you should

leverage. It's what gives them their Voice. With anything they say

or write, they are creating music. Look for the signatures that

make them unique.

I will even go further and look at them from a

demographic and psychographic angle. Where are they from?

What makes them tick? What makes them emotional? What

are they passionate about? How are they to me? Who are they

to other people? Who are they trying to be? If you understand

them on a higher level, you will write for them on a higher level.

For example, when writing for an MTV show, the target

was teenage girls, so I read teen magazines, like Seventeen and

Twilight. I made notes about the music they were listening to,

the slang they used, the shoes they were excited about, the boys they thought were cute. I captured all of this in a profile that

helped me see their world outside my own. This profile brought

the person to life for me. It made me consider their daily lives,

their passions, their traits, their struggles — not just what we were

trying to say, but what they wanted me to say to relate to their

lives. It all gave me perspective. It made me consider things I

could have never considered before. And, I could look to it

often to remind myself of this person I'm writing as and for. I

could add to it and evolve it as they too evolved in this world.

3) Invite Them In

Writing in someone else's voice is not about getting outside of

your own mind. It's about inviting someone else in. It's about

being able to hear their voice inside your own head so they write

for you. To do this, let your head be an open room with only

them in it. Based on your research and profile, give them an

anchor phrase that demonstrates their patterns and character — a

sentence that perfectly captures them. With everything you

write, hear that phrase in your head, in their voice, to show you how to write what's next.

For example, I used to write for a sports announcer — Wes Johnson, The Voice of the Washington Capitals. His voice is legendary, and so to get it right in writing, I'd listen to recordings to invite his unique voice into my head. After a while, I would pick up on the way he'd use syllables in a unique way. There was a code in there, and when I listened long enough, it became apparent. I boiled it all down to one thing that inspired every word I wrote from there on out. It was only two words — Washington Capitals — but I could hear it in my head, over and over (I still do), like how he would lengthen and build the word Washington to increase tension and excitement. Then, everything I would write would be driven by that key phrase in order to match his patterns, to sound the same, to sound like it actually came from him. He spoke clearly in my head and the words were therefore his.

Dumb Writing Tip #20: Get another POV.

There you are, you're Braindumping, trying to figure out what you want to say, what you want to communicate. But, you got nothing. You can't think of other perspectives or ideas. That's ok, it happens. Sometimes you just don't have the time or mental capacity to find new ways of looking at things. So, when you don't have thoughts of your own, steal someone else's — not through plagiarism obviously but through the quick reading of ideas in the comments section of online articles. There are some real gems in there! With the digital wall separating people, they feel free to share their thoughts and ideas openly, even when they damn well shouldn't. Take advantage of that. Find blogs and publications around a similar subject you're writing about, and then find someone debating or building upon the topic. In the comments section, people argue and boldly take a stance on a subject. They always seem to think they're the absolute subject-matter expert, and when everyone is the expert, it makes for some fun arguments. But, through it all, you pick up different perspectives and ideas. Read through each one and consider other ways of looking at the subject you're writing about. By doing so, it expands your perspective and provides fuel for more multidimensional writing.

Dumb Writing Tip #21: Don't overthink it.

I've already said it, but I know you didn't listen. No one ever does. And so I repeat: Don't overthink it.

Write that down on a post-it and put it somewhere you can see. Make it your mantra. Tattoo it onto your wrists. Whatever you have to do to remember to not overthink your words and writing, do it. Your brain's insecurities and belief that because it can process information it should do so incessantly is holding you back from connecting yourself to the world through writing. Yes, it is that simple. Yes, you do it every day. Yes, you can overcome it. Just don't overthink it. Just be a bit dumber.

What A Wonderful

Time to Write!

"Don't forget — no one else sees the world the way you do,

so no one else can tell the stories that you have to tell."

- Charles de Lint

As a Writer, you're powered by your past. Your experiences,

your opinions, your adventures — they all fuel your words. Yet,

you struggle to get words onto the page. You overthink

everything and make excuses. You don't see that you have a

world view that's unique and powerful, just waiting to be

unleashed onto the page. Because of everything you've seen,

done, read, heard, felt, and the generation in which you exist,

you're a member of the most fortunate generation in the history

of mankind, and you don't even know it. And, it's not just

because of what you have now, but because of what you didn't have when you were a kid when you were careless, and curious, and you didn't overthink, or overplan. This is the secret to writing with Heart.

As a child, you followed your Heart, always. It was a magical time in your life, wasn't it? Ideas flowed naturally. You wrote for fun, even if it was in crayon. Stress, anxiety, work-life balance, self-confidence — these were not topics of conversation. Instead, as children, we climbed trees, we took things apart, and we fell down a lot. We created without blockers or judgy eyes around us. We grew up in a time when our playtime radius stretched miles. We looked at hills and forests, wondered what might be on the other side, made up stories, and adventured out there to places that represented possibility and personal expression. Our parents pushed us out the door and told us not to come back until dinner, or until we were bleeding. We'd swim great distances, build things with our little hands, and give our own unique meaning to things we'd discover.

We had TV, but we couldn't sit too close to it, and we certainly couldn't take it with us. Sure, we also had Gameboy, dial-up, and Oregon Trail to entertain us and spark our sense of imagination for a time, but they were novelties, sideshows to what really mattered. We were the main event in our lives each and every day, because we didn't have access to constant, ever-changing entertainment, unless it was the entertainment we created within our own minds.

But now, we live in a world of daily innovations, developments, and breakthroughs. We are witness to the great transition into a fully digital age where information and content are commonplace. It's never been easier to be a Writer, to share your words, to connect with others! The sad fact is, despite this flood of inspiration, so many of us have become numb to the things that could once fascinate. We look deeper and deeper every day into space and discover Earth-like planets so often, I'm not even sure if I'm supposed to be excited anymore. We access books through Amazon or Audible so easily the books lose power. We write on Medium so often the numbers become meaningless, and we read so many articles there that we stop paying attention or remembering any of it. How could we ever hope to compete against the thousands of aimless Medium writers, especially when we can see them so clearly writing in this vast room with us?

We have access to nearly all of the world's knowledge, and we can even attach it to our wrists, but we risk forgetting how exciting it all is without something to compare it to. So, we will have to look back on our wild youth when our imagination ran free. We must reach deep inside our memories to find a true sense of wonder. That is your charge, because we're fortunate to be able to remember a time where when we didn't know something, we asked, we sought, we explored, we made it up. We didn't accept excuses, and we didn't make them. We were never too busy, or overwhelmed, or scared to bring our ideas to life. We just got to work and never called it work. We didn't know the meaning of the word, literally.

Now, everything we could ever want to know is a simple Google search away but we, and only we, still have the power to wonder beyond these technological advancements — something we can't be sure will survive with future generations. We're the last to grow up without the internet, so only we truly know the awesome power of those little information machines we carry with us everywhere we go. We'll likely be the last to actually drive cars with our own physical bodies, so we'll be the last to truly know the personal freedom of the open road. We'll be the last to have gotten lost without GPS, discovering a sense of adventure and accomplishment in finding our way home. And, we'll be the last to experience the power and emotion of a developed photo, whether we waited one hour or even longer. Instead, our memories are to be forever outsourced to social media where they're no longer our own. Those single photos of our youth, which encompassed so much emotion, are now replaced by 100 digital options easily captured and just as easily forgotten.

There's great value in our growing access to technology, of course. Skype meetings and Slack chats, for example, save us and our employers time and money, but you know what I truly miss? Getting to the airport early during business trips, disconnecting, and having a beer while watching the strange mix of people passing by, and wondering about their stories—what strange adventures they might be on. It's a moment I experience less and less each year as technology makes travel unnecessary, but when I get the opportunity, it will always be something I savor and enjoy. I have the past, and you do as well, but others may not. It's a potential extinction of experiences, so you must recognize it, and be present. You must use it to power your words, because someday others may not have this power that you possess.

As more information and innovation become commonplace, and the more we absolutely know and can easily achieve, uncover, and possess, the less we experience, the less we wonder. So, never forget your device-free youth, and your sense of imagination. Never forget the power of child-like perspective. Never forget what it's like to make up your own stories. Never forget that those stories are in you, just waiting to be written.

Embrace your curiosity and imagination, and rediscover the ever-changing world around you. We're the last to experience so much discovery, the last to wholeheartedly

wonder. We're the Wonderful Generation, a fortunate flicker in

existence with the ability to experience two great ages in human

history, so don't let those last remnants of a forgotten analogue

past disappear without letting them influence your eager view of

the future. Unplug whenever possible, wander, wonder, and

maybe listen to some birds. Let everything inspire you and your

writing, every wonderful day.

Words Are Magic

"Words are, in my not-so-humble opinion, our most

inexhaustible source of magic. Capable of both inflicting

injury, and remedying it."

—Albus Dumbledore

One day, as I pretended to take notes in a meeting, I watched

my hand moving across my notebook and noticed something

odd. With slight, unconscious movement of my pen, magic was

happening. Symbols, shapes, ideas were coming to life, bleeding

forth from my pen, and they evoked further meaning, emotion,

wonder in my mind. I wiggled my pen on the page and images

were born in my brain. Incredible! This was no small thing. This

was something unbelievable that I'd simply never paid any

attention to. I realized I wasn't merely spelling words. I was

doing something wonderful. I was casting spells. It was magic.

And I'm a magician!

Crazy? Maybe, but only if you underestimate words

themselves, the strength of them strung together, or our ability to wield them. Words can make your heart beat faster, make you sweat, make you cry, make you fall in love.

Consider that words are of the supernatural sort, other-worldly, yet not; gifted to us by some divine spirit, maybe; ever-changing, not ours, simply floating in us and around us, shaping our world and each other, but still shaped by our own innate, internal passions and energy—our blood!

Sceptical? Well, you can explain words as well as you can explain magic, and it'd be just as fun hearing you try. That's because neither are driven by truth, but by belief. Our acceptance and understanding are not bound by logic, but by emotion. We believe in words, we breathe life into them, we cast them into the world and they thrive. But, when we stop, when we abandon them, regardless of their linguistic evolution, regardless of their past, they die. They exist to communicate, to express meaning and understanding, to serve as a symbol for something, and then...poof, they're gone. (Magic.)

In fact, the word 'spell'—to spell a word—actually influenced the idea of casting a spell—to use magic to influence others. And, it had such magical power over me after observing my notebook scribbles, I went so far as to learn more from my favorite wielder of words and Yale professor, Dr. Mike Zimm (editor's note: James and Zimm sit next to each other, so James "magically" just looked over and asked). Zimm said (immediately and without research, because he is a huge nerd), "The root 'spellam' originally meant 'story, saying, tale, history, narrative, fable' and then the term 'spell' started to take on the meaning of a charm or magical incantation in the Middle Ages."

See, told you: huge nerd.

"In the Indo-European tradition, words were viewed as having magical abilities, or possessing a dangerous magic," Dr. Nerd rambled on. "For example, the daughter languages of Proto Indo-European arrange the consonants in the root for the animal 'wolf' in bizarre ways. This is probably because the original speakers — before 3000 BC — feared that if they said the actual word for 'wolf' it would magically cause the animal to appear. It's the origin of 'curse words' — the belief that the usage of particular words had powerful negative effects — the ability to curse yourself or others. And, it can be seen in M. Night Shyamalan's movie *The Village*, in which the villagers refer to the creatures they feared as 'Those We Don't Speak Of' as well as in *Harry Potter* where characters refer to Voldemort as "He Who Must Not Be Named.'"

Once again, big-time nerd.

So what does all this magic talk really mean? Well, for Writers, it means we're magicians; we're powerful. We can cast spells over the world by spelling words into existence and we can change the way people think, feel, and act. That's our ability as Writers, speakers, and storytellers; that's our gift—to influence others, to create the unexpected, to change the way people see and understand the world, to put on a show.

Consider the power of one word alone. A single magical word can not only change something's meaning, it can convince someone to change how they think.

In 1974, an experiment was conducted in which people were asked to recall what they'd seen in a car crash video. Some were asked if they'd seen "the" broken headlight and some if they'd seen "a" broken headlight. Those who were asked if they'd seen "the" broken headlight were three times as likely to have seen it than those in the other group. Truth was, there was never any broken headlight in the video.

A single, small collection of letters created a memory people believed was true! They reported on something that never even existed. Yeah, you got it, it was Magic.

Still don't believe in the power of words? Finish this sentence:

"What if..."

Oh, the endless places those simple words, those six letters, can take you. The sparks of imagination burning in your brain this very moment. Your imagination, like a child's, explodes with unrestrained possibility. What if you could use that very power of inspiration, creation, and connection with everyone you meet? Answer: you can.

We wielders of words, we sorcerers, charmers, creative conjurers, magical beasts; we are free to spell words into existence at will—writing that's crafted to convince, to change, to instill a sense, a feeling in someone beyond their control.

There's real power there. We are undoubtedly unstoppable.

For new Writers, the ones who want to be but haven't yet earned the title, take note: these powers are not held by professional Writers alone. It's in you, right now! We're ultimately talking about the brain—our endless canvas, where words live and breathe—and it's open to all.

Artists, designers, strategists, thinkers, and any sort of creator in this world, you've made it this far, so I have a gift for you: you, as well, are magical. You too have the power to create thoughts, feelings, and imagery in people's minds in your own way. You speak, you write, and you think, so you are unstoppable, as well.

How? By using your passions and craft to tell stories. You are human and therefore you are a natural storyteller. It's built into you. You can control minds with those stories. You do it for yourself without realizing. Every night your stories give you an escape, letting you play in fantasy worlds. You go to bed and your brain sits up telling itself wonderful stories, both memorable and mundane.

Never forget that you are here today because mankind has spent thousands upon thousands of years developing the magic of communication and stories. How dare you not believe in it. How dare you not believe in yourself. How dare you not open your soul and share your magic with others!

Never forget that those who truly believed in their magic—who dedicated themselves to wielding it in new, powerful, exciting ways—they will live forever. Tell me that's not magic. Never forget that you are a force of nature with all the power of the universe on the tip of your tongue. Words are mankind's greatest creation; capable of transcending time and space; capable of controlling the human mind; capable of anything.

You can do anything. You don't just have your life to control, or progress, write, or rewrite. You have ever world imaginable, and as yet unimaginable. As a writer, you have the unique power to create new worlds and shape them as you see fit. That can scare you and you can do nothing, or it can empower you. So, embrace words and their power. Imagine the unimaginable. Create for the sake of creating, for inspiring. Read, write, tell stories, wield your magic. Be a magician.

Write With Blood

"He who writes in blood...does not want to be read,

he wants to be learned by heart."

—Nietzsche

Another way to express the process and ability of writing with Heart over Head is doing so with Blood. That's because talented Writers and creatives have something beyond skill that cannot truly be explained, harnessed, or diagnosed. It's a deep, emotional hunger to make, dissect, understand, share, destroy. It's our ability to transcend education and experience to somehow craft new things and new worlds. It's our ability to do something with Blood.

To do anything with Blood—with passion—is to be skillful, deliberate, and precise with your actions, and to not simply follow all the right steps and rules, but to put yourself—all of you— into the work. Whether you're a Writer, a designer, a painter, a developer—or any doer, maker, believer—you can go beyond simple step-by-step structures and established processes to create something immensely powerful and unforgettable.

As a professional who strings words together for a living, I believe that writing with Blood is to write with spirit, to feel the energy in you and around you, and to funnel it into your work. It means including everything that is you; the best and the worst parts of yourself, all there, right on the page.

Call it divine frenzy, poetic madness, a drunken outburst, or simply inspiration (from the Latin inspirare, meaning "to breathe into.") Whatever you call it, our power is a gift that is breathed into us and can never be shared or truly explained. Simply, our Blood is our innate talent. Skills can be learned, but our natural ability, our irrational spirit, the Blood for the work, can never be taught.

This natural, savage style of work, and our passion for it, thrives on uncertainty. If we always knew what it would look or sound like, we'd be too bored to complete it, so we must stumble over ourselves for a time in order to truly create. We must embrace our curiosity and imagination and reach out into the darkness. We must open a vein and bleed.

If we don't bleed, our work, our world, becomes a tired exercise of habit and commonplace. We find our routines and our style, and we repeat, repeat, repeat. Someone who doesn't write with Blood becomes a tourist to the work. They go to the same old, uninspired places. They become predictable, hitting the spots everyone expects them to hit. They're never truly seeking new worlds, or looking to create them. They aren't sneaking down back streets to discover the mysterious and unknown. They aren't creating truly unique experiences.

Sure, powerful experiences, crafted by talent, can be finely curated and perfected over time. But, they're hardly special, and rarely memorable. As a creator, you must be willing to take the journey your work demands. You must answer its call, abandon preconceived beliefs, and be willing to go places you've never dared explore before. Because, that's where greatness lies.

"Be daring, be different, be impractical, be anything that will assert integrity of purpose and imaginative vision against the play-it-safers, the creatures of commonplace, the slaves of the ordinary."—Cecil Beaton

Writing with Blood is to misbehave. Tell a creative it's already been done, and they'll gladly find a different way to do it. That's because where we see disorder, we wish to create order. Where we see harmony, we wish to create chaos. It's up to us creative minds to break the rules, to ask what's next, and to find connections between strange, unexpected things.

To write, to create, to design, to play, to do anything with Blood is to escape yourself in order to disrupt routines, expectations, and most of the trivial things you've been taught. It's not a kicking and screaming disruption of the work, yourself, or the world around you, but a disruption of the way you look at the work, yourself, and the world around you. I believe deeply that repetition limits our creativity, so we must bravely disrupt conformity with every opportunity, and resolve the struggle of defending our own beliefs in the face of others. We all seek acceptance, but first we must accept that our individual beliefs are unique and our own, and we must rebel from expectations to find our way—the way we truly believe in.

To write with blood is to admit, at least to yourself, you're wrong. Assurance in your work breeds stagnation, and stagnation perpetuates mechanical thinking. If you're not admitting you're wrong, or that you can go further still, you're not looking at things differently enough to learn. So, adapt to and seek new changes and possibilities. Strive even in your pursuit of failure. Always dare mighty things without trepidation. To quote from a great adventurer of world and thought, "Far better it is to dare mighty things, to win glorious triumphs even though checkered by failure, than to rank with those timid spirits who neither enjoy nor suffer much because they live in the gray twilight that knows neither victory nor defeat."

By simply abandoning these fears and negative, dispirited feelings, we are actually activating our brain to truly create. Creativity is a neurological process, so when you create, the prefrontal cortex of the brain is suppressed, which is linked to conscious self-monitoring. One part of the brain turns on, and the other turns off. What that means is if you allow yourself to self edit (on paper or in-person) while creating, the creative, magical part of your brain, is turning off. Actively trying to prevent yourself from making a mistake or follow rules means you're no longer creating new perspectives or putting your full self into the work. You're a machine that is willingly turning itself off precisely when you're supposed to be working. You're disabling your own machinery, and for what? To not embarrass yourself? The result is willingly forgoing your right to perspective, and to the pursuit of fresh thinking, of new ideas.

On the subject of perspective and new ideas, Oliver Burkeman wrote:

> "We see the world, and our work, through countless lenses of assumption and habit—fixed ways of thinking, seeing and acting, of which we're usually unconscious. And that's exactly as it should be: Our brains are wired

to automate as many processes as possible, thereby freeing up resources for the unforeseen...You'd never manage to order a burrito—let alone write a novel or complete a redesign—if you had to think consciously about every step. First open your mouth; next, get your tongue in position to form words; then activate your vocal cords..."

In my not-always-so-humble opinion, creativity comes from the self, you, the individual. But, my guide to the spirit world of creative magic, the aforementioned Liz Gilbert feels the opposite. Writing about the power of divine creativity in her powerful book *Big Magic* and detailing the history of the spiritual influence in her insanely inspiring Ted Talk, Gilbert attributes the "Blood" of many artists to be the "geniuses" of ancient Rome and the "daemons" of ancient Greece, amongst other spiritual beings throughout time and space. They're the magical entities that carry with them a creative power, and invisibly assist us mortal artists and creators in our work —

whether in our studio walls, in our minds, or floating through the wind. The artists of the past, and of Gilbert's world, possess the mysterious powers of a "divine attendant spirit that came to human-beings from some distant and unknowable source for distant and unknowable reasons." In fact, with the Renaissance, the artist was not only regarded as one of genius, but by fanciful names, like "the Divine Michelangelo."

Gilbert goes on to discuss how by associating the work with a disembodied spirit, the creator can disassociate themselves from their emotional connections, thus avoiding the crippling effects of certain critique and potential failure. Or, it does the opposite by disconnecting them from the just-as-crippling over-inflation of ego that comes with success. This is a valuable perspective in overcoming the sensitive nature of us creatives. After all, we tend to be serious drinkers and addicts in order to combat the emotional ties to our work, and the constant unsympathetic examinations from the world.

Whether you believe it's a heavenly spirit, or you yourself, your Blood is the power to create. You simply have to harness that energy, that emotion, that spirit, and focus it into your work. Forget your fears, and the oncoming critiques. Prevent yourself from being haunted by mistake or failure, or from realizing you're not truly as great as you've told yourself before the work's created.

Place your trust in your Blood, and it will guide you. And remember, this rare power works for you. It is you. You control it, inspire it, cage it, or let it loose. It is your soul, and your disruption of your world is your ability to channel it toward mighty things. Now's the time for you to create, to open a vein and bleed, and to leave behind the expected. Remember to not just write, but to put yourself into it. Bleed! Live through your work. Give it life. Give it a pulse.

Write with Blood, always. That happens by putting yourself into the work, emotionally and even sometimes physically. It often looks like clenched teeth and a wry smile. It comes with hysterical, maniacal laughter, bouts of talking to one's self, occasional convulsions, and often unstoppable tears. Sometimes you say you're writing with Blood with lots of dramatic exclamation, including a wee little jig and some stuff being carelessly thrown up into the air. If you need a clear visual example of Blood, watch Freddie Mercury perform. However, it does manifest in so many ways, so find yours. Find what makes that act of writing something magical. Find the work no one else could create because it's so unmistakably, unabashedly you. You know you've found it when, at the end of the day, you reread something so mundane as your work emails for pleasure. You notice all the little things you did — little bits of clever writing that probably only you will pay any attention to, but the mere fact that they now exist out in the world is just fucking amazing, isn't it?

Writing With Your Head

"Writing is thinking.

To write well is to think clearly.

That's why it is so hard."

— David McCullough

Good writing is just good editing, and with the Head, this is where you edit all that crap you Dumped out earlier. If writing with Heart was about creative madness, passion, and emotion flowing freely from your veins, then writing with Head is about process and order. It's about thinking through your words effectively and efficiently, without ever *over*thinking them. It's allowing your brain to work without softening it through fear, insecurity, ego, excess thought, and all the other shit up there mucking up your words. It's not about being smarter, it's about simplifying — actually dumbing things down and working through it with intention, so that you may process all that you dumped out with Heart. It's the linking of ideas, not the writing of new ones. Now, at this stage in your writing process, your logical side takes over and puts the puzzle together.

Another way to look at it is that writing with Heart was about planting trees. You were deep in the dirt, never thinking about what this little tree might do or become. You were in the moment, freewheeling and care-free, planting as many trees as possible and trusting in them, believing that some will eventually grow into something great and lasting and some may not, but it wasn't for you to worry about that day. You just worked, never demanding the trees to be a finished, fully-grown that day, as you should never have expected your Braindumpings to be complete when they hadn't even had the chance to be nourished. (Wow, this is a dumb metaphor. Let's continue.) Now that you have a field of saplings, writing with Head is stepping back to observe and manage your growing forest. It's time to be methodical, and decisive, because sometimes you'll have to cut trees back.

Sometimes you'll notice that they never grew at all, that they had no place in this forest, that they were never a tree at all. They were weeds, sucking the life from your trees and overcrowding your forest, and it is time for you to remove them. (Yeah, dumb metaphor, let's move past it.)

If the Heart is writing, then the Head is editing and rewriting to be more realistic for your medium and audience. It's the process of taking what you have Braindumped and polishing it into something worth sharing — getting you closer to done. Before, your effort was to write freely and openly in order to capture many options, ideas, and feelings, and now your effort is to carefully select and cut your ramblings into a tighter form. Without that Heart writing, the pages now would be blank, and you can't fix blank, you can only fix bad.

Writing with Head is where you consolidate and consider structure, format, and the reader. It's where you can rely on style and rules of grammar or you can entirely abandon them. If the Heart was about dumping out 100 things, the Head is about finding the few pieces that actually work, that add value and express what you intended to communicate, and then stringing them together into a cohesive structure and flow.

Though the Heart can be excessive, resulting in you, the Writer, producing way too much content in your Dump, most of which will likely never even be used, the simple effort of creating this excess makes the Head's job easier. It can focus on making it clear and connected, instead of having to suddenly think up a few more ideas, or clever ways to say it. The more time you spend trying to be clever, the more time you waste. Write dumb, not clever, and clever will find its way through somehow.

In the Head phases of your writing process, you have it easy. The load has been lightened. You were creative before, and now you don't have to be anymore. You can relax and simply fix that pile of crap that is your Dump. To make it easier, you can even templatize the rest of your journey, putting your work into traditional formats, like Joseph Campbell's "The Hero's Journey" or Kurt Vonnegut's "Shapes of Stories." Whatever is practical and thought-out works here. This is not a time to imagine new things, it's time to focus your efforts into a completed work.

With structure, you can create anything. Your Dump was a flood of thoughts, ideas, and emotions, but without structure, it is nothing. With Head though, you can take it and craft a song, a movie, or an email — anything! — because all those things are only differentiated by their structure and format. Take a 100-page Braindump and cut it into a 3-minute song, and then a 1-page poem. It's all the same thoughts, ideas, and emotions, only structured differently. The Heart is still in there, but you've used your Head to edit it differently for how you want the world to consume it.

(Uh oh, watch out. Another stupid metaphor is coming your way!)

Think of writing with Heart and Head like a reality TV show. They shoot those things for weeks, if not months. They capture everything with their many cameras — as much as possible. Oh so much of it (if not all of it) is absolutely trash, like your

Braindump. But, then they edit it. They chop it all up, move things around, throw things away. They stop trying to constantly create new ideas, and they simply focus on what they have. They give it structure, and drama, and meaning to all the footage they've shot. They do one thing and then the other, not both simultaneously, because you can't edit what you haven't shot, and you don't have a show just because you shot something. That's why your time writing with Heart was to provide as much footage as possible. Now it's time to edit your show, or whatever it is you're writing, into something that's worth paying attention to.

The value of separating Heart and Head — one and then the other — is in your ability to focus, and not randomly jump between thinking and feeling, writing and editing. That back-and-forth only disrupts your flow and results in confusion and a gnawing internal debate over your words, resulting in blocks and unfinished writing. The controlled nature of the Head, and its reliance on guidelines and structure, allows you to focus not on what could be, but what will be. It is now that you focus on finished. So, separate and simplify, write with Heart, edit with Head, and you will write better, faster.

Dumb Writing Tip #22: Find self-control in simplification.

Writing with your Head is about simplifying and clarifying. By doing this, you're restraining yourself and your creative efforts so that things become clearer, more achievable, and your stress decreases. You are slowing down the frantic nature of your Heart with simpler, focused tasks. To do this, make the moment clear in terms of what you're doing, where you're doing it, and how much time you're allowing. And, be honest with yourself. You're going to be a lazy bum. You're only human. Allow yourself a set time for "research" (scrolling mindlessly on the internet as you inevitably procrastinate) but when you are past that time, there's no more. There is no Wikipedia, no social, no Google. Focus. You're done "researching," it's that simple. Straight-up unplug your router if you have to.

This self-control is important because when overwhelmed with options (like the endless nature of the internet), we tend to regret our decisions later, obsess over foregone alternatives, continuously find new distractions, and constantly go back and fix what doesn't need to be fixed The result is that we tweak and overthink our writing forever, and never ship it or share it with anyone. Instead of accepting that right now you need to be editing, you start daydreaming and thinking up new options. Instead of accepting where you're at, you're consistently going backwards and overthinking things you've already thought about. But, you're not doing this because it needs to be overthought, you're doing it because moving forward into the unknown is scary. And, all of the Braindumping, notes, thoughts, and ideas look like a lot of work, and that's even scarier. You're allowing your lack of structure and focus to derail you from finishing your writing. Remember, done is better than perfect, so keep your eyes ahead and edit what you have toward completion. Simplify, simplify.

Research actually shows that the more 401(k) plans people are presented, the less likely they are to sign up for any at all. Similarly, when faced with an abundance of stock investment choices, they avoid the market altogether. With too many options, we become paralyzed. The same is true for the writing process. When you can do anything, you do nothing. So, simplify and focus. Avoid having to make countless decisions. Give yourself structure and a simple task to accomplish. Ask yourself, "What am I doing right now?" Then do that one thing only.

"I am researching"

"I am explaining things to myself like I'm an idiot."

"I'm Braindumping my flow of consciousness."

"I am listing random things."

"I am editing and consolidating my research into something manageable and structured."

"I am re-reading for flow, context, and content."

"I am now proofing."

All of these make up the writing process, but are simpler,

focused, digestible steps that help eliminate the great fear that comes when you consider all of the options, decisions, and possibilities that come with crafting words. You're not doing many things; you're doing one thing. You're not editing while writing, and vice versa. You're allowing your Head to control your Heart, which sometimes needs to be done. And, along the way, you'll discover simple solutions to complex challenges. When you've done it, you'll tell yourself that it can't be this easy, that you didn't actually write anything, but that's exactly the sort of focus and flow you're looking to achieve in your work. Don't overthink it.

Dumb Writing Tip #23: Stop chewing things over.

I can see you, sitting in front of your computer, thinking, not writing. You're letting words and ideas float around your head in endless circles. It's exhausting, for both of us. And, fun fact: this loop of thoughts that keep you from writing can actually lead to anxiety and depression. In the world of mental health, it's called Writer's Rumination, named for the "chewing over" of thoughts, much like how a cow consumes its food — chew, swallow, regurgitate, and chew again, just like your ideas.

This rumination process burns time, energy, and contentment, leading a Writer to focus more on the possible negative outcomes: "What if I don't finish? What if I never get there? What if no one likes it?"

It's inevitable, but there's something you have to remember: you can't truly control your writing, especially when you need the writing gods to breathe inspiration into you. And, you can't control time or another person's reaction to your work. What you can control is your own mind. You can stop it from getting stuck trying to predict the unpredictable, or control the uncontrollable.

Writing with Head is about controlling your own mind. It's about reminding yourself that you're in charge, that the work will get done, that the ideas you have already are enough to move forward. Writing with Head and, more-so, writing dumb are about limiting fear, stress, and anxiety, all which stem from rumination.

So, keep your eyes on the page, trust in your Heartfelt Braindumpings, and do not try to predict the outcome. You are here, and this is the path forward.

Dumb Writing Tip #24: Support yourself.

This writing tip is in no way dumb, and yet I feel dumb every time I use it, most likely because I'm worrying too much about what others think of me and my writing process. It's is a technique to keep you focused on your world, to eliminate negative rumination, and to infuse small amounts of motivation and inspiration through words. It's to surround yourself with post-its and other notes that inspire and support you. Literally surround yourself with words to allow yourself to live, temporarily, in a world of words where you feel safe, comfortable, and inspired. If you aren't feeling confident, put confidence-building messages around you, like "You are the best writer at this desk." It's true, isn't it? If you're struggling to write in a voice or style, put examples around you that represent that style, like romantic, flowing poetry if that's what you're working on, or teen slang if that's your audience and voice, or both when writing romantic poetry for teens. I once even kept the worst headline I ever saw smack-dab in front of me to remind myself that, at the very least, I won't write the worst headline in history.

Whatever will help you in any way, rely on those words. Create the environment that best supports you as a Writer.

Editing Your Dump

"I'm not a good writer. I'm a good editor."

— Jason Rose

So, now you've got this big ol' Dump of writing that is ugly and seemingly meaningless, now what? Answer: You finally turn it into something useful.

The Braindump is a shotgun approach to writing — a massive untargeted projection of all the possibilities that you could consider. The edit process of this method is to recognize all of the puzzle pieces you have laid out before you, and you begin carefully putting them into place. It's where you begin to see your intended work finally take form. A Braindump could be a song, a novel, a movie — or all of the above. It all depends on how you shape it. You don't write a movie; you write a story. You just edit it into a movie during this stage of writing — you give it acts and screenplay formatting. The same can be said for an email — you give it a greeting and a question or call to action.

In both cases, and anything you might be writing, you have rationale intention (yours, a character's, the reader's, and all of the above), as well as elements of Heartfelt personality and emotion. With all of that, you want to create a resulting thought, emotion, or action in the reader — to think, feel, or do. In your writing, regardless of its medium, you want to communicate through story and language in a way that incites something in someone. You want to take them on a brief journey with your words, feeling a connection across space, time, and pixels. All of this truly happens here, in the edit. Remember: there's no difference between writing a movie and an email, except the time and structure you provide it. At the core of anything is intention.

Oftentimes, when I'm at this stage of the writing process, someone will ask to read my first draft. The challenge is that I generally consider the Dump and all subsequent forms of it through this process to be my first draft, and rarely are they friendly to other people's eyeballs, but that's ok. The Dump was for the Writer, and so is this. It's all still a vast collection of all of your ideas and intentions, and once filled, you and you alone will start to feel the flow of what it will become. Obviously, no one else would be able to, but it's for you, not them, anyways. So, tell them to shut up and wait — you're writing!

However, even though this is your first draft, do not use your Braindump as the place you're actually writing the final piece. The Braindump is sacred and should exist even after you're done with it. This is so you can go back to reference the Dump, or to get more information — a helpful link, quote, or thought. If you try writing in the Dump itself, you will start overwriting everything you've done up to this point. You will lose valuable ideas and research in an effort to begin cleaning up and finalizing. If, in an editing frenzy, you chop something from your Dump, it's an idea lost forever, and now is no time to be thinking of fresh ideas — you need to focus on moving forward. To lose all those wild, imaginative thoughts from before would be simply wasteful. That's why it's time to expand your Dump into multiple forms. Copy & paste, duplicate, create the same thing many times. Each Dump will serve a purpose. Be comfortable having many tabs and drafts open at once. Be ready to confuse yourself around which one is which, but remember that it's better to have multiple drafts than to lose the work you've already done by deleting something now that might be useful later.

Separating your Dump into multiple forms allows you to better process all that crap you collected. If done right, your OG Dump is likely many pages long, with different fonts and colors, creating a colorful mess that would be difficult for anyone else but you to digest. And now, you have to dive in and start figuring out what your idiot Heart came up with. You have to start wading through the excess, pulling out the gems and piecing together bits of writing that are already complete.

To begin your edit, remember to always have a true Dump that remains intact — you never edit in here — and then move everything to another edit document where you can work from. This is not even your final draft document. You'll want one more where final words will end up. That's one Dump, transformed into three documents. Annoying, but worth it.

At this point in your journey, you have:

1. Your Dump: everything goes in, nothing comes out.

2. Your Edit: where you arrange thoughts into sections. Copy and paste everything associated with what you're focusing on in that moment here. When it's a nice cohesive thought, you move it to...

3. Your Draft: where you drop clean, crisp, finalized writing after it's processed through the Edit.

Working in the Edit

The second document, the Edit, is a vital component to the writing process because it allows you to stage and process information as it moves between the creative Braindump stage and the final drafting.

With an editable version of your Dump here in this document, you can begin trimming excess — deleting things you've collected but are no longer relevant. These might be quotes, stats, ideas, or just mindless ramblings, but at this point, you may feel that you don't need them anymore. By deleting

them from the Edit, you can start to simplify and focus your

Dump in order to get closer to done. Plus, by having the first

Dump intact, you can delete from the Edit freely, knowing you

can easily retrieve those words again, if needed.

As you delete from the Edit, you can also begin moving

things around. You'll notice similar thoughts and ideas, and how

they support one another or build upon each other. For a

movie, it might be things that go in the same scene, or act, or

maybe it's elements of a character that once grouped together,

you're better able to reference who they are as you write their

scenes. For a school paper, it might be the same arguments for

comparing and contrasting. All of these comparable elements

you can move around in your Edit to be closer together. This

allows you to start bucketing information in a way that begins to

resemble your intended written piece. Also, feel free to start

naming these buckets or describing them, whether at the

beginning in bold or as a comment. It helps to process lots of information when you know what big blocks information are, roughly.

Example:

- *"This is the introduction, because it explains what I'm writing without too much explanation, because I want people to still read the damn thing."*

- *"This is my first half of the book, all about Heart, and here are all the things that support it, like Writing With Blood"*

- *"This is the second half of the book, all about Head, and here are all the tips on structure and style — the boring shit."*

- *"This is a bunch of random stuff, which I don't know what to do with, I'll force them in later and hopefully no one will notice it's out of place."*

Regardless of what it will end up being, by bucketing, you may begin to see the structure and shape take form. You might begin to notice Dump elements that resemble an introduction, or specific chapters, or a great way to close things out later.

Throughout this, you're not writing, you're editing, and you'll find that your brain is far more comfortable doing that — there's less pressure. There is also far less confidence needed in cleaning up writing, as opposed to birthing it from nothing. You're no longer fighting in an arena, you're simply arm-chair quarterbacking from home. Just think about how easy it is for others to comment, edit, and shit all over your writing. Everyone has opinions, but not always fresh ideas, and this stage of the writing process is utilizing that opinion to craft all of the ideas you've collected in the Dump. Plus, it's a calming feeling to know that this thing you're writing is there, right there, in the notes. The hard work has already been done. This is the easy part. It's all in there. You only have to carve and chisel away the excess to find it, like a sculptor who sees the statue in the block of marble.

Remember not to fall back into the Heart stage, unless you plan on staying there. Your brain cannot quickly shift between the two, so if you feel a creative pull back toward the Dump, allow yourself time to play there, but make it clear to yourself that that's where you are. And, if you do switch, create rituals or experiences that reset your mind. Go for a walk, chat with someone, grab a coffee — each allows you to take a few moments to step away from the writing so that when you return you can set a new course for yourself or return to where you were when you were finding yourself straying.

As you edit, with bits and pieces of Braindumpings now coming together, you'll find incomplete half-thoughts and gaps between. Let them exist in their buckets without connecting them until you've fully processed the Dump. You'll want to go all the way through multiple times, deleting what's not useful, bucketing what is, all the while pushing excess down below. You'll quickly notice a clear divide happening: good content rising to the top and bad content falling down below.

Though bad and seemingly useless right now, do not delete the content down below. This might be useful later. Instead, recognizing that the stuff at the top is the best stuff, give it order. Whatever you're writing, it needs structure. The top of your Edit is now your outline, in which the form you want the piece to take is laid out so that everything that remains can simply be placed into the right spot. If it's a movie script, you might have your Inciting Incident and Turning Point. If it's an article, you might have your Lead and use of the Inverted Pyramid becoming clear with the most important information near the top. If it's an advertisement, you might have your Headline, Subhead, Body, and Tag. If it's a website, you have all the different sections or components. Whatever your form, you can certainly find a template online, and then you can copy & paste the good content right into it. Always remember though: a template is a guideline but certainly not a rule. Break the template where you see fit, follow the path you want to take. Otherwise, your template will guide you to something that feels repetitive or overly "cookie-cutter."

Regardless of medium-inspired structure or form, no matter what you're writing, you're telling a story, and storytelling is simple. It's a strange science that — regardless of medium or form — engages and manipulates the human mind. We're born with that gift. It's innate, developed over millennia of human evolution, so trust in your storytelling abilities. But know, despite what many would tell you, your story is not guided by needing a beginning, middle, and end. That's merely a gross oversimplification provided by those who want to sound like they know what they're talking about, and it's a concept that offers no value to you, the storyteller. Your beginning is merely where you decide to begin, and your end is when you're done telling your story, and everything in between is the middle, so obviously there's a beginning, middle, and end. What does it offer? Using a guideline of "beginning, middle, and end" is like saying the winning team in a hockey game is the one with more goals when time runs out — it's ridiculously obvious and therefore beyond dumb to say out loud. We're writing dumb, but we're not that dumb.

Storytelling is simply choosing a destination, where your story ends, but more than that, it's crafting a journey that's actually worth taking all the way to the end — whether it's a movie or that email you're writing. We're storytelling beasts, yet most of the stories we tell each other throughout the day are akin to something like this...

"I was parking but couldn't find a spot. Just when I thought I found one, I started turning in, and a motorcycle was in the spot already."

Sure, it's got a twist ending, but as a story, it really sucks. It also has a beginning, middle, and end, but who the hell cares?

"I was driving down the highway when suddenly a car cut me off."

Bad story, but you've probably told something like it recently. Your mind is desperate to share your experiences. It just needs help making it interesting and worth telling. So, instead of using the "beginning, middle, and end" template, use this one to tell your stories:

Storytelling Structure

1. Connection: draw in the audience, make them care, make them feel like they relate. This can be something they understand, like a normal day or relationship they share, or it can be a shared or understood goal. For example, "I can relate to that farmer's desire to go on an adventure. I'm bored and feel trapped at home. I could use some interesting shit in my life, too!"

2. Obstacle: create tension that threatens to take away the thing your audience relates to, and that makes them want to pay attention to see what happens next. Humans love drama and conflict, so instead of scaring them away, it will likely draw them closer. For example, "Oh no, the farmer and his friends are captured! What will happen next?!?" This tension can also be as simple as stating a problem in an email. The reader is drawn in by the tension and will want to see if or how you will overcome it.

3. Release: relieve them of the tension by providing solutions to the obstacle in unexpected ways. This rush

of relief creates new drugs for the brain to enjoy. And who doesn't like drugs?

Any story, at a high level, does those three things. That is your beginning, middle, and end, except it actually does something. And, if you dive deeper, you will see that within this story structure is the same exact structure, repeating over and over. It's Fractal Storytelling — an endless pattern of story that repeats within itself. Ever trilogy, every movie, every act, every scene, every conversation, every line makes a connection, creates an obstacle, and then releases you from the tension, only to repeat again, keeping you hooked and sparking releases of pleasing drugs in your brain.

Understanding that three-part story structure to push and pull your audience, along with everything laid out into its template and form based on your desired medium, you probably have something that is beginning to look like a final piece of writing, yet it's entirely ugly. The sentences don't connect, the fonts and colors are probably not matching, it's full of errors and mistakes, and it does not flow in any way. That's ok though, because *SPOILER ALERT* the Heart is coming back soon, ba-by!

Dumb Writing Tip #25: Use the inverted pyramid.

No matter what you're writing, you're competing for someone's attention. That's why it's important to give them enough of what they need early so as to provide them value, yet make it intriguing enough that they keep reading. A classic journalism technique for this is the use of the Inverted Pyramid. The wide base of the pyramid, upside down, represents the beginning of your work. Provide them the basics — the who, what, when, where, how — and then compel them to learn more. From emails to movies, effective writing happens when the reader receives your message. Great writing is when they receive your message but are also entertained, moved, and intrigued along the way. The pyramid hooks them and introduces the message. Getting the rest across is up to you.

Dumb Writing Tip #26: Know where you're going.

Know where you want to go and getting there becomes easy. As an example, I'm driving, and you're with me in the car. You are along for the ride, not knowing our destination. But, if I say, "Now, give me very clear directions on where to go," you might wonder, "Well, shit, I don't know where we're going!" You can't get anywhere unless you know where you're going. You'll be writing yourself in circles, never knowing when you're actually finished. But, if I tell you to explain to me how to get to your house, your mind turns on and everything becomes clear. Your home is the destination, it's the completion to our journey. And, that's the point. Know where you are, know where you want to go. Then, plot your course, whether forward or backwards, as long as you complete the two points. That's writing. That's storytelling.

Dumb Writing Tip #27: Use existing structures.

If you wanted to build a house, you're likely to utilize or learn from what others have already done, meaning you wouldn't start from scratch, you'd use a pre-existing house structure and plans.

Maybe it's a colonial, or a Cape Cod, or a rambler, but whatever it is, there is an architecture already in place, which allows you to focus on making the house more of your own through smaller details and modifications. The same goes for writing. There are already countless structures, formats, templates, and examples out there. Why not use those to get started? Why reinvent and redesign a house every single time? Save your creative juices for the important stuff. Fix it later. This Edit of yours is merely a baseline, a blueprint to work from. You can change things later as you see fit, but at least you're building. Your effort is rarely to re-invent the house, it's to design your own. The house already exists and millions have already been created, so use what others have already built as a foundation for your work. That way, you're not solving problems that have already been solved.

Dumb Writing Tip #28: Slow down.

All this nonsense I offer probably doesn't seem like the fastest way. After all, at this stage in the writing process, you've just spent hours, days, or even months doing nothing but putting thoughts onto a page — words and thoughts that may never exist in writing on the actual page! You're writing and typing and researching and seemingly spinning your wheels for what? Maybe nothing, it seems. All that Braindumping and now you have to spend just as much time cleaning up all this nonsense. I hear you, but you're wrong to think that. Remember that we're here to be dumb, to stop overthinking it all, because the truth is that you were always moving forward with your Dump. You were just moving slowly. But, as the Navy SEALs say, slow is smooth and smooth is fast. It's a saying that speaks to how they operate as a team. First, hey do things slowly. Then, they learn to be smooth and methodical and precise until they better understand their process. Once they've done that they can become fast. It's no different with Writers. You must be patient and take your time, because no great writing was done in a moment. Slow is smooth, smooth is fast.

Remember this when you are faced with a seemingly impossible deadline. A client might want an ad, or to be rebranded, by tomorrow. You'd think the fastest way to get it done is just to write it, to put it right into a template and hurry it out the door. But then, that's all you have — an unthought-out templated thing you call writing. But, people will know that. They will feel it. You're putting what seems to be all the correct information into it, and you're doing it in a smart, mindful way with your fancy templatization. But, you're wrong, because you think too much and feel too little. That speed will more likely draw you into a rumination cycle, introducing fear and anxiety. The fastest way to finished is not by quickly throwing words into a template, it's to slow down, breath, follow your process, and believe that the journey will get you to where you need to go. Slow is smooth, smooth is fast.

Writing Your Draft

You've dumped with Heart, edited with Head, and now you come back around again with more Heart to creatively put the pieces together with flavor. This is where you take the formatted and structured mess at the top of your Edit and move it into your Draft document. Now, all that remains in your Edit is all the seemingly useless junk down below. This remains in case you need to build on something later. Everything still exists in the Dump, but this excess in the Edit becomes an edited-down, unused collection of thoughts and words for you to consider using later.

In your Draft, the Heart returns to find creative solutions for bringing the ideas together and to life. Your effort is to build upon what is there, not remove or delete. You have a basis to work from, and can see what the structure will ultimately be, so now you use emotion and energy to write yourself closer to the final piece, connecting dots, building upon ideas, adding flourishes — making it sing! Don't think about grammar, spelling, or rules. In fact, don't think at all; just feel the writing, listen to the little Writer in your brain, and go where it takes you.

So much of the work has already been completed, so now you can infuse more Blood and energy to the work, considering things like alliteration, anaphora, chiasmus, and other valuable rhetorical techniques that hook your reader, while creatively linking sentences, ideas, and paragraphs together so as to make the entire piece work together. Now, you're building upon what already exists to find the real music in your writing. You're taking seemingly disparate ideas and finding a through-line that connects it all. That singular line that links them, beginning to end, should tie back to the one thing this was all about — that singular thing that started this journey. It guided your Braindump, but also make sure it comes through in the final product as well. It is not to be abandoned. You ideated toward one clear goal, so if it's no longer valid, then all of your upfront work is no longer valid. If it's an email trying to get a client to sign off on something, every touchpoint, sentence, question, or joke should be tied together with a thread that ties your email to your intention. This is where you see how Heart and Head are separate yet one within each other. As you build upon your draft, infusing magic, Blood, and energy into the writing, you are also carefully considering the focus of the piece using your Head. You are doing one thing (writing with Heart), and not the other (editing with Head), yet each is at work in a mindless, unintentional way.

Dumb Writing Tip #29: Give yourself credit.

So simple, so dumb, but so effective: just put your name on the top of the page — your byline — to remind yourself that you are the Writer and no one else. Take credit and take pride in what is happening. This is your space to fill, no one else's. It's your vision, your voice. The reader will take the journey you lay out for them, so if you give them nothing, they get nothing. That's daunting. But, by seeing your name on the top of the page, it's a constant reminder that you are in charge of this journey.

Finalizing Your Draft

With the writing elevated through Heart, it's time to put the creative mind aside in order to finish your draft with an edit and polish. This is where you can, if you want, finally worry about grammar, spelling, and any rules you might be breaking. This is also the boring part, and one of the most difficult aspects of the writing process because your brain will inevitably fail to see all the mistakes you made. So, put the work aside for a bit, or get someone else to help proof and edit your writing.

Even though now is the time to consider the rules of writing, don't overthink it. Get it out to that other person to read, review, and edit. If you try to make it perfect before you do so, you will never get there. By sharing your writing, you're forced to accept that it is not, and never will be, perfect. So, accept that you made mistakes. Accept that even though you have spell-check, it may still be riddled with errors. Accept that there are countless rules and writing concepts that you don't know — nor should you. You are most likely not an English professor, and you are most likely not writing for one. Neither you nor I will be honored in the halls of Yale or Harvard. Who cares? Don't worry about imperative verbs and oxford commas. Don't worry about semicolons and interrobangs. Just write, and send it out into the world without overthinking it all.

While I'm most often asked about the starting stages of writing, the next most common point is right here — the end. The person has an idea, they've expressed it through written word, and despite working on it, they now believe it to be terrible and embarrassing, so they sit on it. CEO of the brand consultancy Digital Surgeons, Pete Sena, came to me with this very problem. He's a brilliant guy and a brilliant Writer, but he doesn't see himself as such. He's a visual thinker, yet he writes passionately — with Blood. He, however, then leaves the work in an abandoned draft, never to be seen again. He gets in his own way, worrying about what others think about his writing before he even gives them a chance to think about it. When explaining why this was happening, he offered that it was because he was worried about active and passive voice. This is a rule of writing that many are quick to point out, but let me tell you — fuck it. Don't worry about passive voice — just write. If you can express yourself the way you want, and it has a certain ring to it in your ears and inside your brain, then do not worry about things like active and passive voice, or all the other crap. It's quite unlikely the person reading it will notice. In fact, I've been writing professionally for nearly two decades and I'm not entirely sure what active and passive voice are, because I don't care. I don't worry about it, I don't think about it, and no one's called me on it yet. So, be dumb like me. Just write.

Final Tips

Don't let the noise of others' opinions drown

out your own inner voice.

Have the courage to follow

your heart and intuition

— Steve Jobs

You've come so far and whether you're turning an Edit into a

Draft — infusing more of your voice with Heart — or are now

working your way through your Draft — balancing rules of

format with Head — consider some final oh-so-dumb tips to help

you see your work through to the end:

Dumb Writing Tip #30: Feel your words.

Use words you can hear inside your brain. Don't say that

someone spoke loudly, say they shouted. Loudly plays subtly in your brain, but shouting...that you can hear and feel smacking against the inside of your skull. The word itself shouts, so utilize words that evoke imagery, feeling, and meaning.

Dumb Writing Tip #31: Notice notorious mistakes.

The sad reality is that most readers are terrible Writers, which means they don't care about mistakes. However, if you get those few readers that do care, they might, at the sight of glaring mistakes, stop reading altogether. In worse cases, they might not want to hire you or work with you. Simply, mistakes in your writing can result in a loss of opportunity, reputation, and money. But, you know that, or why else would you still be reading a book about writing?

To avoid mistakes, you could get everything proofread by another set of eyes, but that takes time and money, so the simplest way to avoid making mistakes is to just watch the simple stuff that can have a huge impact. Think of those ones you see often that get people the most annoyed: "They're, their, or there? Your or you're? It's or its? Me, myself, or I? Who or whom? Affect or effect?" If you're unsure which to use, just write your sentence another way. It's better to play it safe than make the glaring error.

Dumb Writing Tip #32: Give your writing rhythm.

Writing is music, and everything you write is a song. So, give it rhythm and flow so it can appeal to the audience's ears and soul. Sometimes write long verbose sentences with beautiful points, punctuation, and perspective. Sometimes write short ones. You're the maestro. And, to find this rhythm, try reading your work out loud. Once spoken, you're more likely to hear the music in it. Does it come across as repetitive? Change sentence length, move pauses around, utilize rhetorical techniques to establish patterns that appeal to the ear. Write your song and let it sing.

Dumb Writing Tip #33: Say one thing per sentence.

There have been a lot of One Things in this book. That's because complexity and confusion bog down most writing. We try to jam too many thoughts into every sentence. We rarely give ourselves the time to stop, slow down, and figure out what it is we're even trying to say. And so if your sentence is trying to make more than one point, if it's saying more than one thing, it's most likely bloated or confusing to the reader. Simplify.

Dumb Writing Tip #34: Punctuate properly.

Know the difference between em dashes, hyphens, colons, commas, and semicolons. Google is your friend here. Each piece of punctuation has a specific, correct usage and each is often misused. But, using the correct punctuation allows you to write for the read, to control the speed of the writer. To stop. Consider. And to carry on again as if rushing down a water slide of ideas without stopping. Done right, punctuation represents that elements of communication left out of writing, like timing, a look, a pause, an inflection. So, use punctuation that speeds and slows the read at the right spots. Use those weird shapes to make it human.

Dumb Writing Tip #35: It's not what you write, it's what they read,

Know your reader. Keep their perspective in mind and how they can translate your writing to mean something else entirely. Watch out for multiple meanings in your words, as well as idioms that could mean something more than what you think — especially regional ones. It might sound fine to you, but when you consider how someone else might read it, you might see that it is in fact fairly similar to a popular phrase that offends. For example, if you wanted to express that the words you use really matter, and therefore require consideration and respect, you might say, "#WordsMatter" But, what you might not be considering is that the reader may make an association to the Black Lives Matter cause, and therefore they may see you as trying to downplay their message. What might sound clever to you might be downright insulting to someone else. It's a challenging and confusing thing to consider, but it is your job as the Writer to do it.

Dumb Writing Tip #36: Forget English class.

Focus less on rules and more on the best reading experience. As long as it's a simple yet engaging read, you can break some rules now and then. Though, it's likely the things you remember from class are actually outdated and no longer followed.

Dumb Writing Tip #37: Say what you mean, mean what you say.

Don't use words that lessen your impact. Weasel words like "very," "just," "mostly," "slightly," "seems," "sort of," "pretty," and "somewhat" signal to the reader you mean what you say...but not really. You become a weak, unreliable narrator, so never pull your punches, unless it's part of your plan. Eesh, lots of alliteration there, apologies.

Dumb Writing Tip #38: Write like a human.

Good writing sounds like a conversation, not a lecture. If your reader doesn't like the conversation, they'll stop reading. So, don't make it sound like writing, make it sound like a human voice. Then, the reader will feel you reaching out through the page with your words. That's how someone truly connects with your efforts.

This is a challenge you see most often coming through with brands. Behind them are business, which inherently do not have emotion. However, the people behind it, operating it, do. That's why natural, conversational, non-robotic language ensures the reader can connect, understand, take what they need, and act appropriately — engaging with the brand to help drive the business.

To be more human in your writing, be yourself and have empathy. Be warm, inviting, and personable. Use contractions. Use humor. Use puns, sparingly, please. Hell, use emojis. Use simple words, words people know. Don't make them have to go look up the words you use. You wouldn't want to talk with that person at a party, just as people don't want to read what they write, because it's a chore and it creates more work for them. So, always aim to not only be human, but just a little bit dumber than your reader. Not only do people rarely enjoy having to go look up words but more often than not, they're all-around pressed for time. They turn to quick blog reads or, god forbid, just read the headlines. Be dumber than them. Offer words they know, simply, and don't try to sound clever. Give them what they're looking for, but do so in a fun, engaging way. Don't try to impress anyone, just express yourself.

Often, when people hear that I am a Writer, they automatically assume I use big, fancy words. But, the truth is, I'm usually the first to admit that I have no idea what words mean. I don't know any of those fancy words because I never use them, and I never read the Writers that make me go look them up. I'm lazy, and a bit dumb, and even sometimes surprise myself that I do in-fact know how to read. I only try to express my point as simply as possible. If you have to look up a word I use, then my work is not effective. It's only taking you out of the moment. Mark Twain said it best: "Don't use a five-dollar word when a fifty-cent word will do."

So, be human, be dumb, and don't try to write something profound and fancy. Just write what you're trying to say. Make it clear, make it personal, make it something someone can connect with.

Dumb Writing Tip #39: Stay in your 4-foot world.

Like in climbing, nothing matters but what's next on the rock (or desk), that which you can reach — your 4-foot world. Work doesn't matter. The guy at the base watching you doesn't matter. Looking stupid doesn't matter. Because, no one can help you but yourself. You are here, and all that matters is your next move. If you start becoming fearful, doubtful, or distracted, you fall. If you start thinking ahead to feedback or failure, you've already fallen. All that matters is your next move on the screen. Just like climbing a rock face, writing takes focus and courage, so stay in your world.

Dumb Writing Tip #40: Write for the read.

As it's important for you to write like a human, you must also remember the human on the other side of your words — you must write with empathy. This is more than how they may misunderstand or perceive your words, but also what they want from them.

You might assume they want a hero when they really want a friend, or a teacher, or a rebel. What your writing serves a purpose, so make sure it's fulfilling that purpose.

To help bucket these for yourself and the reader, look at Carl Jung's 12 archetypes. By breaking down these basic models of humans, we can see how they create thoughts, emotions, and actions in others, better enabling us to connect and deliver with our words.

Dumb Writing Tip #41: Design your writing.

The greatest sin you can commit is to create a confusing read. That's why you must design your writing for easy reading at every stage of the reader's journey, regardless of the medium. If there's an easier way to say it, or a cleaner, or more poetic structure, use it. If you can cut words, cut. If you feel you're overusing punctuation but it helps make the sentence more clear, get over it and drop in that damn comma. Like it or not, writing is a visual game. How it appears to a human's *looking balls* is important.

Dumb Writing Tip #42: Get eyes on it.

An obvious one, yet so often it's not done. Why? Because we're too scared, whether we admit it or not. Ask people to proof what you've written and start a dialogue about it. Let them challenge you and your words, but defend them, as well. Having other people read what you've written is key to ensuring that your writing is as readable as possible. Even if you're not done, tell them it's coming to give yourself a deadline driven by peer pressure.

Dumb Writing Tip #43: Let it suck.

Remember to avoid perfection at all costs, and just accept that it will suck to some. That is a great secret of professionals. They've done the work enough to know that perfection is a myth, and criticism is inevitable. The perfect piece of writing is simply unattainable, so they don't even try to achieve it. They seek other goals instead, ones that can actually be reached.

Meanwhile, the amateurs seek perfection, and fail endlessly.

They overthink it, constantly. I know many "writers" who dream

of selling their big screenplay before even finishing it, or

novelists or have 100 ideas but are still fiddling with all of them.

They write, and rewrite, and rewrite, and rewrite, forever. It's

easy to fine-tune something for years, and if that fulfills you, fine.

But, if you want to make a career of this, if you want it to last,

and you want to pay your bills with it, you need to finish, and

you need to accept that it is not and will not ever be perfect. No

matter what it is, someone will hate it, but at least it's done.

Dumb Writing Tip #44: Solve problems one at a time.

Your writing is just a long series of problems and challenges for

you to solve — each aspect a puzzle unlike the last. Don't let that

overwhelm you. Focus on one problem at a time. Ask yourself

what the next problem is and solve that one only. If this

sentence doesn't flow, you can't be thinking about what's next,

or if it ends correctly, or if you should use a contraction. You're thinking about all of those challenges, which means you're not fixing the first one. The more you worry about, or try to solve simultaneously, the more time you waste. Simplify, streamline, and don't overthink.

Dumb Writing Tip #45: Make this your aircraft.

You're the Writer here, the pilot, and this is your plane. This is on you now. You're in control, no one else. Do not wait for anyone else to inspire you, or to give you the answers. Stop reading blogs. The words aren't out there on the internet, they're in your brain, so go ahead, put them on the page. Do it now. Take control. Just write.

To make the situation "your aircraft" comes from the famous plane crash into the Hudson River, where pilot "Sully" Sullenberger is reported to have taken control of the cockpit, plane, and situation by firmly stating to the panicked crew, "My aircraft." But, for me it came not from a disaster but from a success. A designer I've worked with named Matt Pringle delivered an overwhelmingly successful creative presentation.

Now, Matt is a quiet riot of a designer, meaning he crushes pixels, but isn't the first to jump up and deliver a whole spiel to try to sway a room. Instead, he prefers to focus on the work, and let it speak for him. But, not this time. This time, he performed confidently and precisely. He delivered a happy client, a sold idea, and the assurance that we would get out of the situation "alive." Afterwards, I asked him what got him there, what fueled him and empowered him. He answered, "I told myself that this was my cockpit." He went on to explain that he told himself that, out loud, to remind himself that he owned the room, that people would listen to him, because he was the expert and no one else could fly that plane but him.

So, he as you write, tell yourself that you are in control. You are the Writer, the creator, no one else. You are in control. You have to fly this thing, so make sure people feel like you know where you are going. Make sure they can sit comfortably and enjoy the ride. For Sully, lives depended on him. For you, every word, every character, every idea dies if allow it. This is your aircraft, your cockpit. So fly the goddamn thing.

Dumb Writing Tip #46: Don't worry about your audience.

I've already told you to consider the audience, and while certainly true, it's also entirely untrue. Before you can write for other people, you have to be able to write for yourself. That means trusting in your decisions and abilities, and finding a simpler path for putting words on the page without putting too much pressure and worry into what you write and how it will exist to others. Is this a contradiction to other things I've offered? Absolutely, but writing dumb has layers; it contains multitudes.

Being overly self-conscious and being overly conscious of others are both ways of overthinking. At a certain point, you simply have to shut up, stop thinking so much about everything and if it makes sense, follow your instincts, and just write. As Ray Bradbury said, "Anything self-conscious is lousy. You can't try to do things. You simply must do things." And that guy was an okay Writer.

Dumb Writing Tip #47: Stay in your time zone.

At any moment, every day, and even on a grander scale in your work and career, each of us in our own time zones. There are those who are ahead of you, those who are alongside you, and those who are behind you, and it will always be this way. Only worry about what goes on in your time zone. Never compare yourself to anyone else, and never compare your writing. Never look back into history, and never take your age into consideration. All you can do is focus on your own path, and work in your own time.

Dumb Writing Tip #48: Know, love, & believe.

When it comes to anything creative communications, you must engage with the work. That is true in writing, as it is in music, singing, design, and even public speaking. To fully engage with the work is to fully engage with your audience. To do this, you must always do these 3 things:

1. Know the work: Do your research, use your brain, don't start until you're ready. Look at it from all angles, and spend time with it. If you don't know what you're doing or talking about, it will become clear very quickly.

2. Love the work: Use your Heart and feel a connection to what you're doing. If you do this, people will feel it too. They will see the humanity on the other side, and they'll feel what you felt. If you don't, they will see that it is heartless, and they will move on.

3. Believe in the work: Believe that this is worth doing, and that this is a conversation worth having, or else why waste your time doing it? I've read too many damn articles that are listicle garbage meant only to have me click and scroll past ads. They wanted me to give me nothing, and they didn't care if I receive anything. They only wanted my time, were reluctant to even chase after that, and it showed in the sad writing that will never be referenced again. They are dead pixels floating around somewhere. That writer did not believe that this time together, me

and their words, was valuable. Why not believe that the thoughts, ideas, and feelings existing inside your brain, when captured in written form, can bring you together with someone in another part of the world, in another time? This work we do is magic; this time we have together is precious. Believe in it, and in yourself, and in this connection you have created, and your words will carry more meaning.

Dumb Writing Tip #49: Be a Writer.

This one seems obvious, yet more often than not, it's not done. If you want to be a Writer, there are two very easy and very specific things you must do. There are no exceptions to this. Absolutely none. Hold on to your fucking seats because this is the secret behind every single professional Writer. You MUST:

1. Read. Read everything. Read often. Study the craft. Find new ways to do write by seeing what others have already discovered. Find out what you hate by reading shitty

writing. Can you imagine a musician that never listens to music?

2. Write. I always ask interviewees what they wrote this week. Most of the time, they didn't write a thing. They're always taking a break. That's how I know not to hire them. They don't actually like writing, apparently, or else they'd write. Some deeply, passionately want to be a Writer, while others feel it's a path to a paycheck. Either way, if you want to do it well, you have to practice. You have to put energy into something as small as an email. Being a Writer is not something you declare, or a title bestowed upon you, it's something you earn through writing. You might feel the Writer inside you, but you're not one until you actually write. Then you have to get better at it, and share with people. If you work hard enough, someday someone will either pay you or call you a Writer. I know this is a profession for me because at the end of the day I go back and read the emails I sent. I get little bits of joy from the way I structured

them, or added little comedic twists. I notice my sentence lengths or how I flowed between paragraphs. I find my mistakes and cringe. I feel proud of something as small as a damn email, and it makes me happy to remind myself that, because I'm a Writer, doing what I love. So, you want to write or have to write, write, and find the writing that lights you up so at the end of the day you can say you did it, you did it well, and you damn well know it.

<u>Dumb Writing Tip #50: Break all the rules.</u>

"I found that total creativity involves

a certain intellectual rebellion --

not to become a criminal, but somehow,

to be totally creating, you have to do things

that are a little bit forbidden."

- Philippe Petit

"I aim to misbehave." It's both a nerdy pop culture reference

from the movie Serenity as well as a nod to the Oscar Wilde

quote, "A writer is someone who has taught their mind to

misbehave."

That's why I found it fitting, as a nerdy writer, to not only

breath it into my work but to put it right on the top of my

business card. The company I work for encourages the team to

put quotes onto their cards that reflect them and their work.

They are always professional, and clever, and respectable. But,

that didn't feel very me. So, while others were putting clear

work-focused lines, like "I take the lead," I felt the need to rebel,

to actually misbehave, and do something completely different.

After-all, I'm in the creativity business, and doing things

differently is in our nature.

As creatives, we've always felt compelled to fight against

what is expected of us. In school, we cracked jokes and were said to be "disruptive." We kept our heads down and silently sketched in our notebooks, and were labeled "disobedient." We skipped class and went out to see the world, and were called "deviant." We embraced being different, and made it our life's work.

Now, as professional rebels, we strive to be the outsider with the big, shocking idea or the game-changing innovation. We find our worth in seeing things differently and making a show out of any moment. We find our power in embracing experimentation, challenging conventions, and searching the great unknown.

Tell a creative it's already been done, and they'll gladly find a different way to do it. Because, where we see disorder, we wish to create order. Where we see harmony, we wish to create chaos. It's up to us creatives to break the rules, to ask what's next, and to find connections between strange, unexpected things. It's what they pay us for.

But, our biggest hurdle is the place where we get it all

done; our schools and workplaces. It's where rigid structures, processes, and rules are made to guide us, but inadvertently pose the risk of crushing our creative spirit. The more restrictions placed upon us, the more we fall in line and find a comfortable routine, and the less we explore. So here we are, in this crisis of creativity, where the rules and guidelines are stifling; where imagination has been sucked out in place of streamlined progress; where short-term deliverables supersede long-term happiness, thought, and success.

And so, we must remember that rarely were rules we abide by actually made with us in mind. We must become accountable for ourselves, our work, and our words. We must consider what we do when the rules, processes, and dictated approaches conflict with what's right in our writing — what we feel to be right. We must stop thinking and just follow our Hearts. Because, when the rules are such that we can't achieve our individual and collective goals, we simply must rewrite the rules, or break them altogether.

Without taking these risks every day, we risk

dissatisfaction and a numbing of our skills, so fight against groupthink and conformity, embrace your inner rebel, and go break some goddamn rules already.

Choose what you want to use and accept from this book. Use all of it, use none of it. Just fucking write. Break all the rules and write. At the heart of creativity and writing is rebellion. So don't just write, misbehave. To write is to misbehave, it's to block out all the crap in your head. It's to confidently, definitely, and foolishly give the world a middle finger, to say, "I got this, I can do this better, I am not ashamed or worried what you think of me. I will bleed. I will lay it all out for you to trample on if you so wish. I will spread my dreams under your feet. Do your worst."

And because this is all about misbehaving, good writing is feeling like you're doing something a little bad. The only rules you should follow are your own. Ignore those who say you aren't a real Writer. Make your own process. Ignore anything I said if you think it's actually, truly dumb. The only absolute rule of being a Writer is to misbehave, to do things your own way, to be true to yourself and your voice, saying to hell with everyone else and everything around you. This is your aircraft, you are the Writer, no one else. You have a perspective that no one else in the world can offer. So let's hear it. Be bold, be daring. Let the creatures of the commonplace play it safe, it's time for you to go misbehave.

Embrace Your Dumb

"Two things are infinite: the universe and human stupidity;

and I'm not sure about the universe."

— Albert Einstein

I'm going to go out on a limb and assume you didn't read

Voltaire's "The Good Brahmin" because why would you have? I

read it by accident once. It's not bad, but it sure ain't a beach

read.

In it, our boy Voltaire poses the question of where

happiness comes from: ignorance or knowledge? To ask

questions — to understand and develop knowledge — is to reveal

the flaws in the world, each other, and in ourselves. To ignore —

to simply let live and exist — is to be content with our existence.

So, where does happiness come from? I don't care, and this is

the wrong book to discuss it. But, what I do care about is which one makes a good Writer. And, the answer is that good writing comes from both — to be both ignorant and knowledgeable. The Heart allows you to be the ignorant old woman, at peace with what is, free to enjoy, express, and experience. The Head allows you to ask deeper questions, reveal meaning, deconstruct, and to be uncomfortable and discontent but forward moving. The good life of a Writer is to be both, to possess all qualities, but to be bound by neither.

However, as Charles Darwin wrote in his book *The Descent of Man,* "Ignorance more frequently begets confidence than does knowledge." While there is a place for both Heart and Head in our work, we cannot allow one to overwhelm the other. We cannot allow Heartfelt, illogical expression to create a sense of overconfident wisdom in our own self. We must always embrace our stupidity while having the knowledge and wisdom to be aware of it.

As David Dunning wrote in an article for Pacific Standard, "In many cases, incompetence does not leave people disoriented, perplexed, or cautious. Instead, the incompetent are often blessed with an inappropriate confidence, buoyed by something that feels to them like knowledge."

Writing dumb is about becoming unaware of the world around you, forgetting that failure is possible, not worrying about critics and opposing ideas. It's about creating, not critiquing, because your mind can only do one at a time. It's about admitting to yourself that you are neither perfect nor a genius, and that you will without a doubt make hilariously stupid mistakes, but it doesn't matter, because none of us are geniuses. But, it's also being aware that you are doing these things, that though you are ignoring the world in order to free yourself from its judgement, you are still aware that your work is worthy of judgement and not in any way perfect. We cannot allow our intentional ignorance to become our self-confirmed knowledge. We cannot allow ourselves to think we're better at writing than we really are. We cannot get ahead of ourselves (like writing a book about writing — eesh, what an egomaniac, amirite?!?).

To further explain how we must be aware of our own stupidity, consider the Dunning-Krueger Effect — a type of cognitive bias in which people believe that they are smarter and more capable than they really are. To put it more simply, it's when people are too dumb to realize that they're dumb.

The Dunning-Kruger Effect was an administration of tests around humor, grammar, and logic, finding that participants scoring in the bottom quartile grossly overestimated their test performance and ability. In one study, Ivy League undergraduates took a grammar test. Then, after completing the test, the students estimated how their ability to "identify grammatically correct standard English" compared with others. Like the overconfident idiots we experience every day, particularly every single person on the internet, the lowest scoring students of the tests grossly overestimated their abilities. Those who scored at the 10th percentile rated their grammar abilities around the 67th percentile. In essence, their actual grammar ability was really poor, but they thought they were in the top third of students. Idiots. Meanwhile, some of those who tested better embraced their own ability to fail — to be stupid and wrong — and therefore estimated they scored lower than they in-fact did.

In an era of fake news, where our social media networks feed us only what we want to find, we're all brilliant, informed experts with thoughts and words worth sharing. Dunning-Kruger results in our own difficulties in realizing our own incompetence — how unskilled, uninformed, and unaware we truly are — leading to inflated self-assessments, in whatever format that occurs. In the words of Writer Jason Rose, "Once, we knew little but understood everything. Now, we know everything but understand little." The only way through the mess is accepting that we are fools and endeavoring to understand more — to write dumb, but strive to write better, which is probably why you're reading this book. It's to look at a blank sheet and be ok with the fact this will not be the best, but I will be happy to complete it. It's only after accepting our dumb, and embracing it, that we are free to discover truth, in the world, each other, and ourselves.

So, accept you are not as smart as you think you are, and allow yourself to just be. Dumb is good, as long as you know you're dumb.

This rationale acceptance of our own ignorance and inability is also why "non-writers" are often capable of being exceptional Writers. They do not get too caught up in rules and comparisons to greatness, because they either don't know them or they don't care to think about them. They only try to express themselves, playing dumb to the fact that the world is watching, and that this is not their craft. They're aware of neither their own ignorance or brilliance. They merely are. I've seen some brilliant copy from designers just looking to fill out a layout. They assumed a Writer would come in with something good, and since they put so little thought and pressure into it, their copy turned out fantastic, maybe even something I could not have written. Excess thought and complication leads to more excess thought and complication. Thought begets thought, which inhibits Heart and creativity.

Because "dumb" often comes with being unaware of your surroundings, unaware of the opinions of others, unaware of complexity, you are, in turn, free — free to experience, free to enjoy, free to be. It allows you to write without insecurity, fear, and anxiety. By being dumb, you can brush off the critics while so many others act and edit before the critics even have a chance to appear. We become so worried of what will be, we never become. To be dumb is to be fearless and mindless. To be a vast, empty canvas, open to any and all ideas. So, be dumb. Trust in yourself and the opportunities in your inabilities. See yourself as brilliantly ignorant, or stupid smart, and never let the blank page be an obstacle. It is an opportunity — an opportunity to express yourself in ways other mediums don't allow, to create something simple yet powerful.

Ask For the Butter

There's an old story in the theatre about a young actor breaking in with one hilarious scene. In it, she was paired with a more experienced actor, and together they would eat a meal during one key scene. During it, and with every performance, the young

actor would bring a wave of laughs by simply asking for the

butter. It was all about timing, and delivery. It was that type of

energetic comedy only found in a theater where you can react to

a live human performer. However, after many performances,

the laughs stopped coming. She would ask for the butter and

where once there was an uproar, there was now only silence.

Worried, she asks her more experienced counterpart for help:

"Why was I getting laughter one night, but not the next?" she

asked.

"You have to ask for the butter," he responded.

"I did, that's exactly what I did!"

"No, last night you asked for the butter, but tonight, you asked

for the laugh."

So, why in the hell am I telling you this and what does it have to

do with writing dumb? I'll tell you. You have to be in the

moment. You have to write for yourself first, not for the

audience. If your words say, "Like me, like me, like me," you

will be utterly unlikeable. You must be aware of the world, yet entirely ignorant of it. Not everyone is going to like what you write, but as long as you're aware of that inevibility, you can find your confidence to be dumb. It's easy to forget that focusing on the result instead of focusing on the execution leads, more often than not, to a failure to get the result. So, be dumb, write dumb, ask for the butter, not for the laugh.

Go Get Dumb

You can accept stupidity and try your hardest to rise above it despite the odds, or you can embrace it and use it as a tool to succeed. Embrace all that is dumb. See it not as negative or lacking, but as something true and natural. See it as a way of thinking, being, and writing, not as an enemy.

Patience with yourself and controlled ignorance is the only way to survive in this world of idiots, so fall in love with that dumb, primate brain deep down in you that wants nothing but to thrive and find its tribe. Your writing is merely the mindless pursuit of survival, whether professionally or personally, whether you like it or not. It's the very innate drive that inspires communication and community — the very essence of human evolution, so start evolving as a Writer and human being. Use these tips, or abandon them entirely, it does not matter, as long as you write.

Writing Challenge

"Let us do these things not to satisfy the 'rules' or to gratify the whims of the pedagogue, but rather to express ourselves clearly, precisely, logically, and directly — and to cultivate the habits of mind that produce that kind of expression."

— Theodore Bernstein

Let me tell you, being a Writer is weird. Not only for the act of it, but the idea of it. It's a weird hobby and an even weirder way to make a living. We put words together and people pay us for it. (Weird) But, there's just something about it—something fascinating, something alluring, something that makes people want to be able to say that they are a Writer.

In fact, people love talking about the craft (and some idiots even write dumb books about it). Yet, all too often I hear from people who are Writers, but not really. They want to be one, but they don't actually write. They love it, but they don't love doing it. They know they can do it, but they simply don't.

(Yeah, this world is the weirdest) For them, though a passion, writing has somehow become an unexplored creative outlet, something they've always wanted to do but will always do later, and therefore it's never done. But, the great truth, the secret to being a Writer, is that it's not hard. You don't have to be smart, as this book proves. Anyone can do it. But, a real Writer can't *not* do it. Writers write, and a lot of other people just talk about it. So, if you want to be a Writer, know that no one will give it to you. You have to write.

So, it's time to become a Writer (or, at least, a better one):

Ready for a challenge? It comes with these short, daily writing exercises (1 hour a day for 7 days). Overall, your challenge is not to write anything for anyone else's review. Your challenge is to write something that no one else ever could — to demonstrate that unique voice and perspective inside you that has been screaming to get out and play; something so...unapologetically you that you can feel proud enough to share with the world regardless of the fact that this is for no one else but you.

You say you want to write because you hear it, you feel it, so now let everyone else hear it and feel it for themselves.

Challenge Day 1:

Articulate Yourself — Of all the writing I do as a Writer, Brand Articulations are the most fun. They're collections of writing that represent, inspire, and transform the brands and businesses I consult with. In a single document, I dictate all marketing efforts moving forward while representing the essence of the brand, its story, and its voice. It's an accumulation of business, strategy, and pure creativity. It's both an unbelievable thrill and an absolute challenge to write them, and every example I've ever seen online is pure crap. The only way to do it is to write with pure Heart, and then ground it by using your Head. It's to humanize a business — something potentially cold and corporate — because no one wants to interact with a business; they want to interact with a human. So, Heart is absolutely required to find the person inside this corporate entity.

So much of writing comes down to confidence —
confidence in yourself, confidence to fail, confidence in putting
yourself out there for the world to shit on. Confidence comes
from knowing and accepting who you are as a Writer. That
means you have to craft your story — both the good and the bad.
You must deconstruct yourself and elevate the greatness.

That's why you're not only going to develop your skills,
you're going to develop your brand as a Writer by writing an
articulation FOR YOURSELF! This is your starting point. This
is you.

What is your archetype, your voice, your positioning,
your story, your mission, your vision, your values, your
manifesto? Pretend you're a brand. How do you articulate
yourself for the world to not only understand you but connect
with you? What stories can only you tell? What makes you
unique?

Pro Tip: On any articulation, I find a piece of writing that speaks
to the Soul of the brand — that One Thing we talked about

earlier — and let it inspire all of the writing after. It's writing that shows the energy of the brand — that brings it to life!

Deliverable: An articulation, as deep and developed as you can get it, in a single Google doc filled with your favorite writing — your Dump!

Challenge Day 2:

Find Your Voice — It's not as hard as it might sound. Sure, a Writer's voice usually comes with time; not because it isn't there, but because they don't know how to find it.

But, you're here because you hear it in you, so now it's up to you to confidently and audaciously dig deep and bring it out.

My suggestion: simply look for the writing that absolutely inspires you, and collect it in a single doc. It can be poetry, song lyrics, movie quotes, speeches, whatever. But, when you collect it all, you can start looking for patterns. You can start seeing the things that get your heart beating faster. You can start applying

what you've learned to your own writing. That collection —
those patterns — they will make up your voice. That is where
your energy lives.

Pro Tip: Don't copy & paste it. Actually transcribe it. Write it
word for word, line by line. You will understand it better. You
will be dissecting it without even realizing it. You will learn from
it. Do this with everything! I have recorded people in my time
who sounded incredibly brilliant out loud only to find out that,
when transcribed, what they were saying, though convincing, was
actually contradictory and meaningless. The action of writing
words down, by hand or by typing, slows things down and
unlocks a part of your brain that is more critical to meaning. As
you develop that part of your brain, you will be a much stronger
Writer.

Deliverable: A long collection of words and ideas from other
people, all typed out by you, all captured in...you guessed
it...that same Google doc — your Dump.

Challenge Day 3:

Be Observant — A major part of writing is observing the world, people in it, and the things they create, and then gleaning insights from it. That's why I want you to take your headphones out, take a walk or observe the world. Consume someone, something, anything, and find an ah-ha Moment—that unexpected realization or discovery of something new or notable that inspires great thought and discussion.

Then, put that Moment in writing and make the reader feel the same power you felt when you realized it. Make sure it's just one thing. And choose what you want to do with that one thing. Maybe it's to inspire people, and maybe it's to inspire yourself.

Take your one thing and dump about it. Everything, anything. Pull from the people above — the writing that moves you. Whatever you do, do not try to structure or edit your work yet. Just let it flow with Blood.

Pro Tip: Do this on paper or screen, not in your head. Talk about things as if you are writing to a friend, but keep in mind that no one has to read your Braindump. Always remember that the simple act of vomiting thoughts onto the page will create a stream of consciousness that is truly your writing voice. As previously discussed, some Writers, like myself, consider it a little person who sits in your brain somewhere and does that actual writing for you. I can't see any scientific reason for that not being absolutely true, so look for them, ask for them, and when you find them, name them, get to know them, let them drive.

Deliverable: A description in the same Google doc of your ah-ha revelation, however long you want or need it to be. Put it all in there. Don't get it right, get it written. Draft now, craft later!

Challenge Day 4:

Rewrite Something Great — Grab one of those pieces of writing from Day 2 that moves you, and that applies to the one thing you're writing. Consider how perfect it would have been if you wrote this instead of them, and then, knowing that the world will never see this, make whatever changes you want to improve it. Literally change it. Sure, it's great, but it's not perfect, and it's not in your voice, yet.

Find the holes. Find where it lacks rhythm. Find where you can infuse pieces of yourself into it. Make it your own. Make it better. Keep this in your Dump. It ties back to your one thing, and now it's rewritten. It's not their writing anymore, it's yours. Let it be an inspiration to keep writing. Remember that you do not have to write everything originally. Great writing is theft because every Writer, like every artist, takes inspiration from the world around them. You do not, and can not, literally plagiarism them, but you can take the Heart, Blood, and music of their writing and let it play you through your work.

Pro Tip: If you're worried about accidentally plagiarising these works, use color coding to differentiate, and then don't just rewrite or expand on the other Writer's work, write about it.

Write how it makes you feel. Write about the use of language, and rhythm, stand out to you. By writing about it, you are more likely to write like it, gently mimicking it.

Deliverable: A single piece of writing rewritten in the same Dump. It started with something you love, but you have now made it your own by finding its weak points, and by letting its magic breathe inspiration into you.

Challenge Day 5:

Give it Structure — Take your Dump as it sits and begin to infuse some Head into it. At this point, it's likely a confusing mess, so start editing it into what you want it to be. Is it a song, a blog, a poem, a movie, a novel? Use a structure and build from there.

Pro Tip: Any writing can be anything, with the right structure. Whatever format you want it to be in, simple Google common shapes, structures, outlines, and formats, and plug & play into it, using your words from the Dump. Some written elements, like poems and songs, are about editing your words and thoughts down, where as other written elements, like novels and screenplays, are about expanding your thoughts to help complete the story.

Deliverable: An Edit doc to go with your Dump, in which you start to see your outline take shape.

Challenge Day 6:

Share Your Writing — I respect the Writers on Medium, even the bad ones, because they at least put themselves out there for little gain. Too often, people see the sharing of work as scary. The truth about blog content is: it's not very regulated. It's not that sacred. It's not that scary. No one is really judging you. There is no great barrier to entry and your reader will likely forget about you within seconds. So, if you have something to say, just say it. Post whatever it is you've been working on, even only a work in progress as an article on Medium — where people can see it — and don't get caught up on what they will think.

Don't think, don't worry, just write — and share.

It can be about ANYTHING. Just write, dammit!

Pro Tip: Some people like to slave over long-form pieces, such as articles, worrying, overthinking, and overediting. The truth behind almost every single one of the articles I've ever written — whether for myself or someone else — is I did too. I overthink it all, despite everything I've offered in this book. I worry about how it will exist online and what people will think of me. I worry about mistakes constantly. I worry if something is too long, or too short. I worry about looking like an idiot. But, the difference is that I then I get so frustrated with myself for taking so long and being overly critical that I just write something quickly and post it before I can stop myself. I accept that it will never be perfect, and I post. I even post it, see how people respond, and then pull it down to edit later. No one seems to notice or care, and I feel better fixing things later. So, do the same thing. Don't overthink it. Just write and edit what you want to say for one single focused hour and run toward the fear. It's not as scary as you think it is. In fact, you'll probably find that there was nothing to be afraid of in the first place.

Deliverable: A short article or post (which can be anything — poem, play, battle rap, whatever), even if only a draft, in that famous Google doc, and then also post that damn thing on Medium. Don't you dare sit on it. Sharing your work will allow you to capitalize that W to become a true Writer. Writers write, but more importantly, they share it out to the world.

Challenge Day 7:

Fight for Your Words — Not long ago, I asked two Writers on my team when they first felt that they were truly a Writer and also comfortable saying so out loud. Both said that it was after debating with me — fighting for what they wrote. It wasn't writing something great. It was fighting for it, believing in their craft so much that they would stand toe-to-toe with me and say they were right and I was wrong.

That's why you're going to let someone not just read but critique something you wrote for yourself. When you're ready, you will have done everything with purpose. That will mean you can defend it. Tell that person to critique it heavily — to hold nothing back. You will determine where to fight and where to learn.

Pro Tip: Believe in your work or no one else will.

Deliverable: Share your Google doc or anything you believe in and wrote with Blood with someone who will challenge you. In fact, find someone so unlike you that you're absolutely sure they'll hate it. Get ready to go toe-to-toe with them. Writing is a contact sport and you only get better by sharing and accepting criticism. You don't have to take it, but you should find out how people are receiving it.

That's it. One week, seven hours, and you're a Writer.

Do you accept the challenge to start writing dumb?

About the Author

From proudly winning a poetry award at the age of six to never again winning an award he was proud of (insecurity, not ego), James Dowd is a sometimes-award-winning Writer and Creative Director with nearly two decades of experience spanning TV production and advertising.

In recent years, going from many quickly-cancelled TV shows at MTV to the adworld of Madison Avenue, James spends most of his time writing and creating for brands such as Kellogg's, Mercedes, Anheuser-Busch, Mars, Sealy, Sperry, Capital One, Diageo, Ford, (Is anyone still reading these?), Kraft, and the NHL. Outside of all that, he spends his time zoning out on hiking trails, neglecting normal adult responsibilities, and hanging out with his mutts, Lucy & The Jeb.

If you'd like more of his annoying ramblings, or would like to book James for a speaking engagement or Writer's Workshop, you can find him at WriteDumb.com.

Made in the USA
Middletown, DE
21 June 2019